Betty Wing

P9-CDS-058

The
Compatibility
Quotient

Also by Steven S. Simring, M.D.
(with Eric Weber)

How to Win Back the One You Love

The
Compatibility
Quotient

Sue Klavans Simring, D.S.W.,
and
Steven S. Simring, M.D.
with William Proctor

FAWCETT COLUMBINE · NEW YORK

A Fawcett Columbine Book
Published by Ballantine Books

Copyright © 1990 by Sue Klavans Simring, D.S.W., and Steven S. Simring, M.D.

All rights reserved under International and Pan-American Copyright
Conventions. Published in the United States by Ballantine Books,
a division of Random House, Inc., New York, and simultaneously in
Canada by Random House of Canada Limited, Toronto.

Library of Congress Catalog Card Number: 88-91992
ISBN: 0-449-90267-6

Cover design by Sheryl Kagan
Text design by Beth Tondreau Design / Mary A. Wirth

Manufactured in the United States of America
First Edition: October 1990
10 9 8 7 6 5 4 3 2 1

To Eric, Kira, and Owen

ACKNOWLEDGMENTS

The original idea for this project (first called the *Divorce Probability Factor*) came from our super-agent, Bill Adler. Without his endless patience and gentle nudging, we would probably still be back on Chapter One.

We owe a great deal of thanks to our two editors, Ann LaFarge and Lynn Rosen, and especially to Bill Proctor, who revised a great deal of the manuscript. The unnamed and well-disguised patients whose stories we tell are the unsung heros of this work.

Finally, we acknowledge our source of comfort and sustenance, Minnie Klavans, who read and reread our manuscript over many summer evenings at Nanjemoy, Maryland.

CONTENTS

III • The Mix of a Marriage

I

An Introduction to the Compatibility Quotient

Is it Possible to Divorce-proof a Marriage?

Our culture has been permeated by a rose-colored, romantic mythology of marriage.

Deep-rooted beliefs about an inalienable right to marital bliss abound everywhere. How often in our therapy sessions have we heard clients say that it's their destiny to "get married and live happily ever after."

Even after they've been devastated by divorce or betrayal, many hold firmly to their illusions. They accept without question the message of the popular song, "Love and marriage go together like a horse and carriage." Indeed, when Tennyson wrote, "Marriages are made in heaven," he voiced a sentiment that probably the majority of American adults harbor today, even if they don't express it in quite the poet's terms.

In most cases, a good marriage is assumed to be something outside the realm of reason and sensible planning. You wait for lightning to strike—or for Cupid's arrow to hit home, as the case may be—and it's supposed to be all love, kisses and cuddles after that.

What if the marriage falls far short of expectations or fails completely, as it often does? The tendency is for the spouses to learn little or nothing from their mistakes. They just get a divorce and continue their search for a perfect mate.

In the minds of many adults, a happy marriage has become virtually synonymous with Ultimate Happiness. Most would agree that occupational achievements and material rewards, without a family or loved one to share the fruits of accomplishment, represent a hollow form of success indeed. So, for the majority of people, the ideal remains an idyllic, long-lasting marriage—one which in some way has been rendered "divorce-proof."

Yet in our work with families as practicing psychotherapists and as university professors during the past twenty years, we've found that the myth doesn't measure up to the reality. In most cases of wedlock, the initial fantasies about marital bliss soon give way to the facts of friction, frustration and a failure of hopes and expectations. What often finally emerges is a form of incompatibility that proves fatal to the relationship.

These two couples reflect the sort of difficulties we've encountered in our counseling:

THE DIVORCE LAWYER'S PREDICAMENT.
A domestic relations attorney (translation: a divorce lawyer) and his wife recently came to us in a last-ditch effort to salvage their marriage. She described their many problems and expressed the fear that their marriage was in trouble.

In capsule form, her story went something like this: Both of them had been involved in extramarital affairs. They constantly argued with each other. She felt he didn't respect her, and she certainly didn't trust him.

While his wife talked, the lawyer sat glumly, looking into space. He didn't contest any of her changes; in fact, he often nodded his head as she made a point.

Finally, he said, "You know, Doc, I've been a lawyer for more than twenty years. I've handled a lot of divorce cases. But by the time they come to me for help, it's too late." Then, apparently contemplating his own marriage, he added, "By the time they come to you, I think it's probably too late as well."

We couldn't deny the truth of what he had said. As he well knew, his legal clients usually sought him out long after any vitality had left their marriages. Love, or even the *possibility* of love, had frequently been replaced by loathing or indifference.

Similarly, when people come to us for marital counseling, there's often little we can do. The die is already cast. We often have to watch with impotent sadness as the marriages of our patients and our students—even those of our closest friends—come apart before our very eyes.

That was the situation with this couple. They had waited too long to act. Even if they had recognized their problems at an earlier date, they would have lacked the knowledge and interpersonal skills to succeed.

The final result: The divergent values, habits and personality traits of this married couple had developed randomly over the years, without any attempt being made to bring the spouses together or mesh them into a single married unit. Consequently, they had been rendered hopelessly incompatible, and so they got a divorce.

CRAIG'S DOMESTIC CRISIS.

Some years ago, we treated a thirty-year-old single man named Craig for problems involving his failure to succeed at work. A gifted computer programmer, he experienced constant anxiety and stress on the job. He lacked the self-confidence to speak up for his interests and communicate honestly and openly with his supervisor when he was being treated unfairly. Craig also lived at home with his aged and crotchety parents.

It took us a long time to help him find the courage to set limits on his parents' interference in his life and to stand up to his boss. But he made progress, and it seemed that our therapy had been relatively successful—so much so that he decided he no longer needed our services.

About a year later, Craig called us in a panic. He had begun dating for the first time in his life, and as a result, a major new set of problems had hit him. He had met a woman shortly after he had stopped seeing us and had married her a month later.

But now he told us, almost in tears, "This marriage was an unmitigated disaster!"

Craig had become acquainted with Michelle at a bar, where she was a cocktail waitress. He made a date with her, and before he knew it, the two of them were sleeping together. Within days, she said she wanted to get married, and by force of sexual experience and a dominant personality, she led him up to the altar.

Craig's parents in effect disowned him, and they refused even to speak to their daughter-in-law. But Michelle couldn't have cared less. She invited all her old party friends to their apartment and kept the place hopping almost every evening, into the wee hours of the morning. Feeling thoroughly liberated by her husband's comfortable salary, she had quit her job and now devoted her extensive free time to enjoying herself.

Yet this was only the beginning of their differences: Craig was deeply religious, while Michelle had never seen the inside of a church. Craig was frugal to the point of miserliness; Michelle made short shrift of their savings and ran up all their credit cards to the limit. Craig liked peace and quiet, but Michelle preferred constantly blaring rock music, punctuated by a regularly ringing telephone.

It seems obvious in retrospect that these two were totally incompatible. Perhaps a little more common sense would have alerted Craig at the outset that this wasn't the girl of his dreams. Certainly, his friends and family had warned him against getting involved with her.

But Craig, who was completely inexperienced with the opposite sex, had responded blindly to the romantic myths about marriage he had picked up over the years. Despite the fact that he was a logical, intelligent computer expert, he threw sound analysis and caution to the winds when it came to love.

If he had just had the tools to evaluate a potential mate, he might have married someone who was more compatible. Then, an enduring, satisfying relationship might have been possible. Instead, he and Michelle were divorced before the year was out.

Such shattered lives come through our offices almost every day; unfortunately, they are just individual illustrations of a much broader phenomenon that's woefully apparent in the statistics: Today, nearly 50 percent of first marriages end in divorce. Nor do the odds improve the second time around. Divorced people who choose to remarry face a 60 percent chance of failure.

The situation seems to be getting worse. At the turn of the twentieth century, only 10 percent of marriages in the United States failed. But from that point, it's been all downhill. By the Second World War, 25 percent of married couples weren't making it; and in the 1950s and 1960s, the failure rate crept up to one-third.

What's the answer to this dilemma of escalating divorce?

The first constructive step is to sweep away the myths about marriage and encourage people to think more realistically about their relationships. This book is designed for just that purpose. We offer a constructive plan, including some hardheaded analysis of what an enduring relationship requires. This book will prevent you from marrying the wrong person and ending up in a failed relationship.

Some have argued that more relaxed alternate lifestyles, including "trial marriages" where couples live together before tying the knot, may improve the outlook for the institution. Yet the most recent studies show that living together before marriage may actually work *against* the durability of the relationship. A study reported in 1989 by University of Wisconsin researchers, for example, revealed that within ten years of the wedding, 38 percent of those who have cohabited before marriage separate. In contrast, only 27 percent of those who marry without living together split up after ten years.

We believe there's a better approach to the divorce problem— one which focuses on a practical, analytical device that we've termed the Compatibility Quotient, or CQ.

The Compatibility Quotient is a powerful tool that describes and weighs a set of risk factors for successful marriage, including behaviors and attributes that are associated with a high probability for divorce. The CQ can be used by singles to evaluate the marriage potential of a prospective mate, or by married people to adjust their relationship along more productive lines.

Marriage is far too important to be entrusted to luck. Romantic "chemistry" means little over a lifetime. But a solid awareness of your aptitude for marriage—and that of your potential or present mate—can help you avoid the pitfalls of a disastrous relationship. Knowing what the risks are can be the first step in laying the foundation for a durable relationship.

On the basis of our research and experience, we've devised the Compatibility Quotient to predict who will make it in a marital relationship, who is bound to fail, and who must take special action to keep his or her marriage from falling apart. This tool will also help you decide whether the adjustments and compromises you'll have to make are feasible—or even possible.

We've found that compatibilities in marriage are dynamic, not static. Seemingly well-matched people who are initially at low risk for a marital failure can change for the worse over time. They may end up in big trouble after children are born or after some other major life event.

Ideally, you should examine your Compatibility Quotient every year. As with an annual physical exam, there's no guarantee against conjugal "illness." But with a clear picture of your marital status in hand, you'll be in the best possible position to take preventive or remedial action in time. We will show you how to avoid bad marriages, and also how to fix good ones that are getting into trouble.

After you've gone through our program step by step, you should know whether a marriage or prospective marriage has a decent chance of working. Armed with this understanding, you can lower your risk of having to confer with divorce attorneys five, ten or fifteen years down the road.

Love is blind, but an understanding of the Compatibility Quotient will give you vision. In the short run, the knowledge you'll gain may be somewhat painful. But it can save you unbelievable anguish in the end.

In the following pages, you'll see that the Compatibility Quotient can be applied in evaluating and influencing a variety of risky personality types and domestic situations, including the following:

- the deceptive "con artist" who never plays it straight with a lover
- the moody, emotional "roller coaster" companion who trades emotional stability for upsetting volatility in personal inter-actions
- the dependent personality
- the person who feeds on anger and argument
- the lazy bones
- the work addict
- the alcoholic or drug abuser
- opposites who are attracted to each other because of some peculiar interpersonal chemistry
- those with some degree of sexual incompatibility
- couples who have widely divergent philosophies of spending and money management
- those who seem to experience consistent roadblocks in their ability to talk to each other
- those in the throes of one of the "danger times" in the history of a marriage

People subject to these and other high-risk influences are often unaware of what's happening to them. Although they may be careful to assess risks in other areas of their lives, they plunge blindly into marriage, completely oblivious to the chance they're taking. We can't count the times that we've encountered patients who are quite attentive to their cholesterol or blood pressure, but who totally neglect a thoughtful analysis of their most important relationship.

We believe that it's possible both to prevent an incompatible marriage and to make saving mid-course corrections after a marriage has taken place. As a result, this book has been designed to help single people who are contemplating marriage and married couples who still have time to assess their risks and minimize them.

So now, to lower your overall risk of divorce, let's determine your Compatibility Quotient.

What's Your Compatibility Quotient?

What are the odds that your marriage—or prospective marriage—will survive?

The answer to this question depends on your Compatibility Quotient, a concrete, quantifiable indicator which is based on three independent factors:

(1) your own personal compatibility profile,
(2) the compatibility profile of your mate or potential mate, and
(3) a combination profile.

After determining your own compatibility profile, you may find you've scored so low that you'll want to take corrective action to change yourself, even if you aren't contemplating getting serious with anyone right now.

On the other hand, if you do have a prospective husband or wife in mind, the second and third parts of the quiz will give you a better idea about whether or not the two of you will "mesh" in a permanent relationship.

If you're already married and you find from these question-naires that there are serious incompatibilities between you and your spouse, there's still hope! Changes for the better can be made, and we'll give you some ideas later in this book about how to achieve them.

Now, it's time to respond to the questions in the first part of this exercise. Then, proceed with the subsequent parts if they apply to you, and finally, you'll be ready to score yourself. We'll let you know how you stand with your overall Compatibility Quotient after you finish the entire questionnaire.

Part I: Your Personal Compatibility Profile

Answer each of these questions about yourself as honestly as possible. Choose only the *best* answer for each question, even if more than one choice applies.

NOTE: Whenever we use the words *your partner* or *the other person* or some similar term, reference is being made either to your spouse or to a prospective spouse if you're unmarried. Also, we've indicated that some of the following questions are intended only for those people who are single. If you're married, don't answer these questions; we've compensated for their omission in the scoring.

1. **How old are you?**
   a. Under 17
   b. 17–19
   c. 20–29
   d. 30 or over
2. **Are your parents divorced?**
   a. Yes
   b. No
   c. No, but they should have been

3. Have you ever been divorced?
  a. No
  b. Once
  c. More than once

4. Do you have children from a previous relationship?
  a. No
  b. Yes

5. How religious are you?
  a. Not at all
  b. I occasionally attend religious services
  c. Religion is an important part of my life

6. Do you believe in "open" marriage, in the sense that the partners should be free to pursue sexual relationships outside of marriage?
  a. Not at all
  b. I believe in behaving pretty much as I please—and what a spouse doesn't know won't hurt
  c. I believe in open marriage

7. How much education do you have?
  a. High school or less
  b. High school or less, but my parents went to college
  c. At least some college
  d. Postgraduate education, and I'm a woman
  e. Postgraduate education, and I'm a man

8. What is your current employment status?
  a. Full-time student (skip to Question 14)
  b. Unemployed, and I'm a woman (skip to Question 14)
  c. Unemployed, and I'm a man (skip to Question 14)
  d. Part-time student, part-time employed (skip to Question 10)
  e. Gainfully employed (go to next question)

9. How many hours per week do you work?
  a. Under 20
  b. 20–60
  c. Over 60
  d. Irregular, varies

10. **Do you consider yourself a workaholic?**
    a. Yes
    b. No, though I am serious about my work
    c. Definitely not—I'll do almost anything to get out of work

11. **Does your job require you to be in close contact with members of the opposite sex at odd or unusual hours?**
    a. Yes
    b. No

12. **Does your job require frequent travel?**
    a. Yes
    b. No

13. **How about your level of job satisfaction?**
    a. I'm very satisfied
    b. Satisfied, but very much under stress
    c. Not that satisfied
    d. Completely unsatisfied

14. **How's your financial situation?**
    a. I'm very wealthy
    b. I have enough to live comfortably
    c. It's tight right now, but prospects are good
    d. I'm always struggling to make ends meet
    e. I'm dirt poor, and it's not getting better

15. **How persistent are you?**
    a. I don't give up easily
    b. I tend to abandon projects when they get difficult

16. **If you're now single: How satisfactory do you consider unmarried life?**
    a. I am quite content, even though I'd like a mate
    b. I can't stand being single
    c. I prefer being single

17. **If you're now single: Have you ever been engaged or planned to marry in the past?**
    a. No
    b. Yes, but more than a year ago
    c. Yes, and we broke up within the last year

18. **What are you willing to settle for in a spouse?**
    a. Nothing less than a "soul mate"
    b. Someone who will meet most of my needs
    c. Someone with potential I can mold

19. **How easily are you provoked to anger?**
    a. I never display anger
    b. On rare occasions
    c. I've got a short fuse—I frequently yell and scream
    d. I lose control and throw things
    e. I've been involved in occasional physical fights
    f. I've hit close friends or family members

20. **How often do you feel depressed or "down"?**
    a. Rarely, and for brief periods
    b. Occasional bouts of despair
    c. Frequently down in the dumps
    d. Frequent ups and downs
    e. Have tried to hurt myself

21. **How honest are you?**
    a. I've never told a lie
    b. I usually tell the truth, except for small white lies
    c. It's important for me to get what I want, even if I have to bend the truth

22. **How trusting are you?**
    a. I think I'm too naive
    b. I trust most people until they fool me
    c. People are dishonest by nature, so you need to be careful

23. **Are you a jealous person?**
    a. I have been on occasion
    b. I'm very possessive of my friends and lovers
    c. I have had jealous rages

24. **I feel that partners in a marriage should stay together**
    a. Till death do they part
    b. Until the children grow up
    c. Until it no longer works

25. How good a judge of other people are you?
   a. Excellent
   b. I'm right most of the time
   c. I've been right more often than wrong
   d. I've made some bad mistakes

26. Do you make decisions impulsively?
   a. No, I'm quite cautious
   b. Sometimes
   c. I've been known to be impulsive
   d. I enjoy acting on my impulses

27. When faced with a serious crisis,
   a. I often panic
   b. I ask for help
   c. I handle it all by myself

28. My family of origin (parents, siblings, aunts, uncles, cousins) is
   a. Large and close-knit
   b. Small but quite close
   c. Pretty much split up

29. If you're single: What is your current living arrangement?
   a. With parents (skip to Question 31)
   b. With my potential mate
   c. Alone or in a roommate situation not involving a sexual relationship

30. I talk to at least one of my parents
   a. More than once a day
   b. Every day
   c. Once or twice a week
   d. Once a month
   e. Almost never
   f. My parents are deceased

31. When it comes to talking about sensitive issues,
   a. I enjoy expressing myself and hearing what others have to say
   b. I get impatient until I get the opportunity to have my say
   c. I have a hard time talking about sensitive issues, and I'd rather listen
   d. I'd rather avoid them

32. Do you enjoy being alone?
    a. I like being by myself
    b. I prefer to be with other people
    c. I can't stand being alone

33. Do you drink excessively?
    a. I don't drink at all
    b. I don't think so, and no one else thinks I do
    c. I don't think so, but my family or friends think I do
    d. Perhaps
    e. Yes

34. Have you ever used illegal drugs?
    a. No
    b. Recreational marijuana only
    c. I've dabbled with cocaine or other drugs besides pot
    d. I've had trouble with drugs in the past

35. Have you ever had trouble with the law?
    a. No
    b. Only drunk driving, nothing more
    c. Only juvenile stuff
    d. I've been arrested, but never convicted of a felony
    e. I've been convicted of a felony as an adult

36. What is your overall outlook on life?
    a. Things generally work out for the best
    b. You've got to take the good with the bad
    c. Life is a continual struggle
    d. If you don't watch out for yourself, you're likely to be hurt

37. What is your sexual orientation?
    a. Completely heterosexual
    b. Heterosexual, but I am occasionally attracted to members of the same sex
    c. I have had occasional sexual contact with members of the same sex
    d. Deep down, I think I'm basically homosexual

38. How adventurous are you?
    a. Not at all
    b. I like to take chances now and then
    c. I love thrills

39. How would you characterize your childhood?
   a. It was very happy
   b. It was pretty average
   c. It was very unhappy
   d. I was abused as a child

40. How did your parents get along with each other?
   a. They got along quite well
   b. Pretty average
   c. They weren't too happy
   d. They fought like cats and dogs

41. Do you have brothers and sisters?
   a. No, I'm an only child
   b. Yes, but all my siblings are the same sex as I
   c. Yes, and at least one sibling is of the opposite sex

42. Tell us about your friends
   a. I have a few close friends
   b. I have many friends
   c. I have many acquaintances, but no one whom I would call a close friend
   d. I am a loner

43. Are your friends married?
   a. Most of them are single
   b. Most of them are married
   c. Most of them are separated or getting divorced

If you're not now seriously involved with another person, go directly to Part IV and calculate your Compatibility Quotient. Otherwise, if you are married or involved with a prospective mate, proceed directly to Part II.

Part II: Your Partner's Compatibility Profile

This section is for the man or woman you are married to or are thinking about marrying. These responses will provide you with an estimate of his or her compatibility profile. For each question, choose only the *best* answer, even if more than one choice applies.

NOTE: As in the previous part of the questionnaire, whenever we use the words *your partner* or *the other person* or some similar term, reference is being made either to your spouse or to a prospective spouse if you're unmarried. Also, we've indicated that some of the following questions are intended only for those people who are single. If you're married, don't answer these questions; we've compensated for their omission in the scoring.

1. **How old is your partner?**
    a. Under 17
    b. 17–19
    c. 20–29
    d. 30 or over
2. **Are his or her parents divorced?**
    a. Yes
    b. No
    c. No, but they should have been
3. **Has he or she ever been divorced?**
    a. No
    b. Once
    c. More than once
4. **Are there children from a previous relationship?**
    a. No
    b. Yes
5. **How religious is your partner?**
    a. Not at all
    b. He or she occasionally attends religious services
    c. Religion is an important part of life
6. **Does he or she believe in "open" marriage?**
    a. Not at all
    b. I don't know
    c. Yes
7. **How much education does he or she have?**
    a. High school or less
    b. High school or less, but his or her parents went to college
    c. At least some college
    d. If partner is female: postgraduate education
    e. If partner is male: postgraduate education

8. **What is your partner's current employment status?**
   a. Full-time student (skip to Question 14)
   b. Unemployed, and a woman (skip to Question 14)
   c. Unemployed, and a man (skip to Question 14)
   d. Part-time student, part-time employed (skip to Question 10)
   e. Gainfully employed (go to next question)
9. **How many hours per week does he or she work?**
   a. Under 20
   b. 20–60
   c. Over 60
   d. Irregular, varies
10. **Do you consider him or her to be a workaholic?**
    a. Yes
    b. No
    c. Definitely not—he or she would do almost anything to get out of work
11. **Does your partner's job require him or her to be in close contact with members of the opposite sex at odd or unusual hours?**
    a. Yes
    b. No
12. **Does his or her job require frequent travel?**
    a. Yes
    b. No
13. **How about his or her level of job satisfaction?**
    a. Very satisfied
    b. Satisfied, but very much under stress
    c. Not that satisfied
    d. Completely unsatisfied
14. **If you are single: How is your prospective mate's financial situation?**
    a. Very wealthy
    b. Has enough to live comfortably
    c. It's tight right now, but prospects are good
    d. Always struggling to make ends meet
    e. Dirt poor, and it's not getting better

15. How persistent is your partner?
    a. Doesn't give up easily
    b. Tends to abandon projects when they get difficult

16. If you're single: How satisfactory does your prospective mate consider unmarried life?
    a. Seems ready for marriage
    b. Very unhappy being single
    c. Seems to prefer being single

17. If you're single: Has your prospective spouse ever been engaged or planned to marry in the past?
    a. No
    b. Yes, but more than a year ago
    c. Yes, and it ended within the last year

18. Does your partner discuss his or her background?
    a. Rarely
    b. Quite openly
    c. Never

19. How easily is he or she provoked to anger?
    a. Never displays anger
    b. On rare occasions
    c. Has a short fuse—frequently yells and screams
    d. Loses control and throws things
    e. Has been involved in occasional physical fights
    f. Has hit close friends or family members

20. How often does he or she feel depressed or "down"?
    a. Rarely, and for brief periods
    b. Occasional bouts of despair
    c. Frequently down in the dumps
    d. Frequent ups and downs
    e. Has tried to hurt self

21. How honest is this other person?
    a. I don't think he or she has ever told a lie
    b. Usually tells the truth, except for small white lies
    c. It's important for my partner to get what he or she wants, even if it requires bending the truth

22. **How trusting is this person?**
    a. Quite naive
    b. Generally trusts people
    c. Highly suspicious

23. **Is he or she a jealous person?**
    a. On occasion
    b. Very possessive of friends and lovers
    c. Has had jealous rages

24. **He or she feels that partners in a marriage should stay together**
    a. Till death do they part
    b. Until the children grow up
    c. Until it no longer works

25. **How good a judge of other people is your partner?**
    a. Excellent
    b. Right most of the time
    c. Right more often than wrong
    d. Has made some bad mistakes

26. **Does this person make decisions impulsively?**
    a. No, is quite cautious
    b. Sometimes
    c. Has been known to be impulsive
    d. Enjoys acting on impulse

27. **When faced with a serious crisis, he or she**
    a. Often panics
    b. Asks for help
    c. Handles it completely alone

28. **His or her family of origin (parents, siblings, aunts, uncles, cousins) is**
    a. Large and close-knit
    b. Small but quite close
    c. Pretty much split up

29. **If you're single: What is your potential mate's current living arrangement?**
    a. With parents (skip to question 31)
    b. With you
    c. Alone or in a roommate situation not involving a sexual relationship

30. My partner talks to at least one parent
   a. More than once a day
   b. Every day
   c. Once or twice a week
   d. Once a month
   e. Almost never
   f. Parents are deceased

31. When it comes to talking about sensitive issues, my partner
   a. Enjoys self-expression and hearing what others have to say
   b. Gets impatient until he or she can talk
   c. Seems to have difficulty
   d. Completely avoids them

32. Does he or she seem to enjoy being alone?
   a. Likes to be alone
   b. Prefers to be with other people
   c. Can't stand being alone

33. Does the other person drink excessively?
   a. Doesn't drink at all
   b. Drinks only socially
   c. I'm not sure
   d. I think so
   e. Yes

34. As far as you know, has he or she ever used illegal drugs?
   a. No
   b. Recreational marijuana only
   c. Dabbled with cocaine or other drugs besides pot
   d. Had trouble with drugs in the past

35. Has the person ever had trouble with the law?
   a. No
   b. Only drunk driving, nothing more
   c. Only juvenile stuff
   d. Arrested, but never convicted of a felony
   e. Convicted of a felony as an adult

36. **What is his or her overall outlook on life?**
    a. Things generally work out for the best
    b. You've got to take the good with the bad
    c. Life is a continual struggle
    d. If you don't watch out for yourself, you're likely to be hurt

37. **Are you concerned about his or her sexual orientation?**
    a. No
    b. I'm not sure
    c. I think he or she has on occasion had affairs with members of the same sex
    d. I'm afraid he or she is basically homosexual

38. **How adventurous is your partner?**
    a. Not at all
    b. Seems to like to take chances now and then
    c. Appears to be a thrill seeker

39. **As far as you know, what was his or her childhood like?**
    a. It was very happy
    b. It was pretty average
    c. It was very unhappy
    d. He or she was abused as a child

40. **How did your partner's parents get along with each other?**
    a. They got along quite well
    b. Pretty average
    c. I don't think they were too compatible
    d. They fought like cats and dogs

41. **Does your partner have brothers and sisters?**
    a. No, he or she is an only child
    b. Yes, but all siblings are of the same sex as my partner
    c. Yes, and at least one sibling is of the opposite sex

42. **Tell us about your partner's friends**
    a. Has a few close friends
    b. Has many friends
    c. Has many acquaintances, but no one who seems to be a close friend
    d. He or she is a loner

43. Are your partner's friends married?
   a. Most of them are single
   b. Most of them are married
   c. Most of them are separated or getting divorced

44. How responsible do you consider your partner?
   a. Totally reliable
   b. Usually does what he or she promises
   c. Occasionally irresponsible
   d. Can't always be counted on
   e. Grossly irresponsible, I'm afraid

45. In our discussions of important issues, my partner
   a. Takes everything too seriously
   b. Can't seem to take anything seriously
   c. Is able to find some humor in most situations

46. When we have a major disagreement, the other person
   a. Usually remains fairly reasonable
   b. Typically loses his or her temper
   c. Gives me the silent treatment or otherwise responds unreasonably
   d. Frightens me

47. I find my partner
   a. Easy to talk to about most things
   b. Often hard to approach
   c. Domineering or overwhelming
   d. Unfairly coercive

48. Before my partner and I became serious with one another, I suspect that he or she was promiscuous
   a. No
   b. I fear so

49. For single people: My partner is still seeing other people, even though we're supposedly committed to each other
   a. Absolutely not
   b. I'm not sure
   c. I suspect so

50. I view my partner as
    a. Too cut off from his or her family
    b. Reasonably independent of the family
    c. Struggling to work out a relationship with his or her family
    d. Overly attached to mother or father

Now, move on to Part III, which contains questions about your combined compatibility profile.

Part III: The Combination Compatibility Profile

For each question in this combination compatibility profile, choose only the *best* answer, even if more than one choice applies.

NOTE: Whenever we use the words *your partner* or *the other person* or some similar term, reference is being made either to your spouse or to a prospective spouse if you're unmarried. Also, we've indicated that some of the following questions are intended only for those people who are single. If you're married, don't answer these questions; we've compensated for their omission in the scoring.

1. **In terms of our earning potential**
    a. The man earns more
    b. The woman earns more
    c. We earn about the same
2. **Compare the two families of origin in terms of wealth and social class**
    a. The man's family is wealthier or of higher social position
    b. The families are about the same
    c. The woman's family is wealthier or of higher social position
3. **How do the two of you feel about change?**
    a. We both can roll with the punches
    b. We both like things to remain more or less the same
4. **Where will or do the two of you live?**
    a. In a city
    b. In the suburbs
    c. In a small town
    d. In the country

5. **In which part of the country do you live?**
    a. Northeast
    b. South Central
    c. Southwest
    d. West
    e. Other

6. **When we make plans,**
    a. We both tend to stick to our commitments
    b. Both of us tend to be very loose about arrangements
    c. My partner is sometimes irresponsible about keeping commitments
    d. My partner thinks that I'm irresponsible about keeping commitments

7. **When it comes to work,**
    a. I wish my partner would work harder
    b. I wish my partner were more ambitious
    c. I think my partner tries as hard as he or she can

8. **For those who are single: How long have you been seriously involved with your partner?**
    a. Six months or less
    b. Six months to three years
    c. Three years or more

9. **On issues of neatness**
    a. We're both slobs
    b. We're both well organized
    c. I wish he or she were more organized
    d. My partner thinks I'm a slob

10. **When we disagree about little things,**
    a. My partner and I are usually able to compromise
    b. We will do anything to avoid a confrontation
    c. My partner often insists on getting his or her own way
    d. My partner usually backs down and gives me my way

11. **When we work on a project together, my partner and I**
    a. Make sure to do exactly 50 percent each
    b. Each do what he or she can do best
    c. Can readily negotiate our respective chores
    d. Argue about who should do what
    e. Avoid working together

12. **Major decisions in our relationship are generally made**
    a. By me
    b. By compromise
    c. By my partner

13. **Do the two of you trust each other?**
    a. Yes
    b. I do, but he or she doesn't always trust me
    c. Not always
    d. We're really quite wary of each other's motivations

14. **When we criticize each other,**
    a. Both of us are pretty open-minded
    b. I tend to be overly sensitive
    c. My partner tends to be overly sensitive
    d. It usually leads to a major argument

15. **At this point, our views about the style of married life that we would prefer are**
    a. Quite similar
    b. Different in significant ways

16. **Our views about spending money**
    a. Are quite similar
    b. Are often very different
    c. Lead to frequent arguments

17. **When my partner and I spend long periods of time together,**
    a. We rarely seem to run out of things to talk about
    b. We sometimes run into dead ends and go our separate ways
    c. We don't seem to have all that much in common

18. **Our skills and talents**
    a. Are almost exactly the same
    b. Are somewhat different, but help fill in for each other
    c. Are different, and bring us into conflict

19. **In terms of recreational activities,**
    a. We're both quite sedentary
    b. We're both quite athletic
    c. Only one of us is athletic

20. **For the most part, our interests are**
    a. Quite similar
    b. Not always similar, but we can compromise
    c. Not that similar

21. **My partner and I come from**
    a. The same religious and racial background
    b. Different religious backgrounds
    c. Different racial backgrounds

22. **Regarding the number of children we think we want, my partner and I**
    a. Are in agreement
    b. Disagree

23. **Our relationship has already been complicated by pregnancy**
    a. No
    b. Yes
    c. Yes, and that's the major reason we have gotten married or are thinking of marriage

24. **My family approves of our relationship**
    a. Yes
    b. Perhaps
    c. Probably not
    d. They're dead set against it

25. **My partner's family approves of our relationship**
    a. Yes
    b. Perhaps
    c. Probably not
    d. They're dead set against it

26. **Physically, my partner and I are**
    a. About equally attractive
    b. Somewhat unequal
    c. He or she is much better looking
    d. I think I am much better looking

27. **Our attitudes about sex**
    a. Are basically similar
    b. Are dissimilar
    c. Are a major point of contention
28. **How sexually attracted are you to your partner?**
    a. Completely turned on
    b. Reasonably attracted
    c. It's a problem in our relationship
29. **How attractive do you think he or she finds you?**
    a. Completely turned on
    b. Reasonably attracted
    c. It's a problem in our relationship
    d. He or she doesn't seem to have that much sexual desire
30. **In terms of physical demonstration of affection,**
    a. We both like to touch each other
    b. We're both pretty reserved
    c. One of us is much more demonstrative than the other
31. **If you're single: Regarding our sexual relationship,**
    a. By mutual consent, we have not slept together
    b. We have not slept together because one of us does not want to
    c. We have slept together, and we're quite compatible
    d. We have slept together, and it's been somewhat disappointing
    e. We have tried to sleep together, but we can't seem to make it
32. **If you're single: In our sexual relationship,**
    a. We initiate lovemaking about equally
    b. The male is usually the initiator
    c. The female is usually the initiator
    d. We haven't yet had a sexual relationship
33. **When it comes to "matters of the heart,"**
    a. We are both incurable romantics
    b. We are both pretty rational
    c. I wish my partner were more sentimental
    d. He or she sometimes accuses me of being too "hardhearted"

34. When it comes to taking charge,
    a. We both want to run things
    b. Neither of us wants to take charge
    c. My partner is usually content to let me run things
    d. I'm usually happy to let him or her run things
    e. We try to share control on an equal basis

35. How confident are you about the choice of partner you have made?
    a. Absolutely sure
    b. I have some reservations
    c. I'm keeping my fingers crossed

Part IV: Calculating Your Compatibility Quotient

Three steps are involved in calculating the Compatibility Quotient for most people:

- STEP 1—you score your personal compatibility profile from Part I
- STEP 2—you score your partner's compatibility profile from Part II
- STEP 3—you score your combination profile from Part III

NOTE: If you are unmarried and are uninvolved with a prospective mate, you'll derive your CQ only from the calculations in Step 1. If you're in this category, simply complete the scoring for Step 1 and proceed immediately to the explanation of the scores that follows the end of Step 3.

In doing your scoring for each question, enter the number of points (corresponding to each answer you gave) in the far right-hand column. Then, total the points for all the questions and calculate your score for that step as directed.

STEP 1: SCORING YOUR OWN COMPATIBILITY PROFILE

QUESTIONS	ANSWERS	POINTS
1	a = 6 b = 3 c = 0 d = 1	_____
2	a = 1 b = 0 c = 1	_____
3	a = 0 b = 2 c = 3	_____
4	a = 0 b = 2	_____
5	a = 2 b = 1 c = 0	_____
6	a = 0 b = 1 c = 2	_____
7	a = 2 b = 3 c = 0 d = 1 e = 0	_____
8	a = 2 b = 2 c = 5 d = 1 e = 0	_____
9	a = 2 b = 0 c = 2 d = 2	_____
10	a = 3 b = 0 c = 1	_____
11	a = 1 b = 0	_____
12	a = 2 b = 0	_____
13	a = 0 b = 2 c = 2 d = 3	_____
14	a = 1 b = 0 c = 0 d = 2 e = 3	_____
15	a = 0 b = 2	_____
16	a = 0 b = 1 c = 1	_____
17	a = 0 b = 0 c = 2	_____
18	a = 2 b = 0 c = 2	_____
19	a = 2 b = 0 c = 2 d = 3 e = 4 f = 6	_____
20	a = 0 b = 1 c = 3 d = 3 e = 5	_____
21	a = 2 b = 0 c = 4	_____
22	a = 1 b = 0 c = 2	_____
23	a = 0 b = 2 c = 3	_____
24	a = 0 b = 1 c = 2	_____
25	a = 0 b = 0 c = 1 d = 2	_____
26	a = 0 b = 0 c = 1 d = 2	_____
27	a = 3 b = 0 c = 2	_____
28	a = 0 b = 0 c = 1	_____
29	a = 1 b = 1 c = 0	_____
30	a = 2 b = 1 c = 0 d = 0 e = 1 f = 1	_____
31	a = 0 b = 1 c = 1 d = 2	_____
32	a = 0 b = 0 c = 2	_____
33	a = 0 b = 0 c = 3 d = 3 e = 3	_____

34	a = 0 b = 1 c = 2 d = 4	_____
35	a = 0 b = 2 c = 3 d = 4 e = 6	_____
36	a = 0 b = 0 c = 1 d = 1	_____
37	a = 0 b = 1 c = 2 d = 5	_____
38	a = 0 b = 0 c = 2	_____
39	a = 0 b = 0 c = 2 d = 3	_____
40	a = 0 b = 0 c = 1 d = 2	_____
41	a = 2 b = 1 c = 0	_____
42	a = 0 b = 0 c = 2 d = 3	_____
43	a = 0 b = 0 c = 1	_____

SECTION A: TOTAL POINTS _____

NOW, SUBTRACT THE TOTAL POINTS FROM 100 TO DERIVE YOUR PERSONAL CQ:

PERFECT SCORE.. 100

LESS SECTION A TOTAL POINTS .... − _____

YOUR PERSONAL CQ .... _____

STEP 2: SCORING YOUR PARTNER'S COMPATIBILITY PROFILE

QUESTIONS	ANSWERS	POINTS
1	a = 6 b = 3 c = 0 d = 1	_____
2	a = 1 b = 0 c = 1	_____
3	a = 0 b = 2 c = 3	_____
4	a = 0 b = 2	_____
5	a = 2 b = 1 c = 0	_____
6	a = 0 b = 1 c = 2	_____
7	a = 2 b = 3 c = 0 d = 1 e = 0	_____
8	a = 2 b = 2 c = 5 d = 1 e = 0	_____
9	a = 2 b = 0 c = 2 d = 2	_____
10	a = 3 b = 0 c = 1	_____
11	a = 1 b = 0	_____
12	a = 2 b = 0	_____
13	a = 0 b = 2 c = 2 d = 3	_____
14	a = 1 b = 0 c = 0 d = 2 e = 3	_____

15	$a=0$ $b=2$	_____
16	$a=0$ $b=1$ $c=1$	_____
17	$a=0$ $b=0$ $c=2$	_____
18	$a=2$ $b=0$ $c=2$	_____
19	$a=2$ $b=0$ $c=2$ $d=3$ $e=4$ $f=6$	_____
20	$a=0$ $b=1$ $c=3$ $d=3$ $e=5$	_____
21	$a=2$ $b=0$ $c=4$	_____
22	$a=1$ $b=0$ $c=2$	_____
23	$a=0$ $b=2$ $c=3$	_____
24	$a=0$ $b=1$ $c=2$	_____
25	$a=0$ $b=0$ $c=1$ $d=2$	_____
26	$a=0$ $b=0$ $c=1$ $d=2$	_____
27	$a=3$ $b=0$ $c=2$	_____
28	$a=0$ $b=0$ $c=1$	_____
29	$a=1$ $b=1$ $c=0$	_____
30	$a=2$ $b=1$ $c=0$ $d=0$ $e=1$ $f=1$	_____
31	$a=0$ $b=1$ $c=1$ $d=2$	_____
32	$a=0$ $b=0$ $c=2$	_____
33	$a=0$ $b=0$ $c=3$ $d=3$ $e=3$	_____
34	$a=0$ $b=1$ $c=2$ $d=4$	_____
35	$a=0$ $b=2$ $c=3$ $d=4$ $e=6$	_____
36	$a=0$ $b=0$ $c=1$ $d=1$	_____
37	$a=0$ $b=1$ $c=2$ $d=5$	_____
38	$a=0$ $b=0$ $c=2$	_____
39	$a=0$ $b=0$ $c=2$ $d=3$	_____
40	$a=0$ $b=0$ $c=1$ $d=2$	_____
41	$a=2$ $b=1$ $c=0$	_____
42	$a=0$ $b=0$ $c=2$ $d=3$	_____
43	$a=0$ $b=0$ $c=1$	_____
44	$a=0$ $b=0$ $c=1$ $d=2$ $e=4$	_____
45	$a=1$ $b=1$ $c=0$	_____
46	$a=0$ $b=1$ $c=2$ $d=3$	_____
47	$a=0$ $b=2$ $c=2$ $d=3$	_____
48	$a=0$ $b=1$	_____
49	$a=0$ $b=2$ $c=3$	_____
50	$a=2$ $b=0$ $c=1$ $d=2$	_____

SECTION B: TOTAL POINTS _____

NOW, SUBTRACT THE TOTAL POINTS FROM 100 TO DERIVE YOUR PARTNER'S CQ:

PERFECT SCORE.. 100

LESS SECTION B TOTAL POINTS .... −

YOUR PARTNER'S CQ .... _____

STEP 3: SCORING YOUR COMBINATION COMBINATION COMPATIBILITY PROFILE

QUESTION	ANSWER	POINTS
1	$a = 0$ $b = 3$ $c = 2$	_____
2	$a = 0$ $b = 0$ $c = 1$	_____
3	$a = 0$ $b = 1$	_____
4	$a = 1$ $b = 1$ $c = 0$ $d = 0$	_____
5	$a = 0$ $b = 1$ $c = 1$ $d = 1$ $e = 0$	_____
6	$a = 0$ $b = 0$ $c = 1$ $d = 1$	_____
7	$a = 1$ $b = 1$ $c = 0$	_____
8	$a = 1$ $b = 0$ $c = 1$	_____
9	$a = 0$ $b = 0$ $c = 1$ $d = 1$	_____
10	$a = 0$ $b = 1$ $c = 2$ $d = 2$	_____
11	$a = 1$ $b = 0$ $c = 0$ $d = 1$ $e = 2$	_____
12	$a = 1$ $b = 0$ $c = 1$	_____
13	$a = 0$ $b = 2$ $c = 2$ $d = 3$	_____
14	$a = 0$ $b = 1$ $c = 1$ $d = 2$	_____
15	$a = 0$ $b = 1$	_____
16	$a = 0$ $b = 2$ $c = 3$	_____
17	$a = 0$ $b = 1$ $c = 2$	_____
18	$a = 1$ $b = 0$ $c = 2$	_____
19	$a = 0$ $b = 0$ $c = 1$	_____
20	$a = 0$ $b = 1$ $c = 2$	_____
21	$a = 0$ $b = 3$ $c = 6$	_____
22	$a = 0$ $b = 1$	_____
23	$a = 0$ $b = 2$ $c = 3$	_____
24	$a = 0$ $b = 1$ $c = 2$ $d = 3$	_____
25	$a = 0$ $b = 1$ $c = 2$ $d = 3$	_____

26	a = 0	b = 1	c = 2	d = 2	_____
27	a = 0	b = 1	c = 2		_____
28	a = 0	b = 1	c = 2		_____
29	a = 0	b = 1	c = 2	d = 3	_____
30	a = 0	b = 0	c = 2		_____
31	a = 0	b = 1	c = 0	d = 2	e = 3	_____
32	a = 0	b = 0	c = 1	d = 0	_____
33	a = 0	b = 0	c = 2	d = 2	_____
34	a = 2	b = 2	c = 0	d = 0	e = 1	_____
35	a = 0	b = 1	c = 2		_____

SECTION C: TOTAL POINTS _____

NOW, SUBTRACT THE TOTAL POINTS FROM 100 TO DERIVE THE COMBINATION CQ:

PERFECT SCORE.. 100

LESS SECTION C TOTAL POINTS .... _____

THE COMBINATION CQ... _____

AN EXPLANATION OF THE SCORING

As you went through the foregoing calculations, you probably noticed that some items were assigned a relatively high numerical value, while others carry a low or zero value.

The reason for this variation is that some factors, like the relative social and financial standings of the two families, are relatively unimportant. On the other hand, other influences—like extreme youth, drug or alcohol abuse, bad temper, workaholism or trouble with the law—are *very* important. So throughout, we've tried to assign appropriate weights to the answers, according to their particular impact on compatibility.

Each of these questions and the point scoring are based on scientific research, our clinical observations or both. For example, you may have been surprised to see that couples from the Northeast have a lower risk of broken marriages than those from other parts of the country—yet demographic studies suggest that this is indeed the case.

Now, for an explanation of your Compatibility Quotient, or CQ:

The CQ is determined by balancing your three compatibility scales. If you're unmarried without a prospective mate, you will use just the first scale involving your personal compatibility profile.

The maximum score on each of the three scales is 100, but we don't expect anyone to achieve such a high result. In fact, a score on each of the three scales of 95 or above would mean you have an *excellent* overall Compatibility Quotient, with an extremely low risk of marriage failure.

If your score was 90 to 94 on each of the three scales (or on the first scale for those who are unmarried and without a prospective mate), your total CQ is *very good*. The odds of your being able to enter into a successful relationship—or to maintain the marriage you have—are excellent. Both you and your partner are ready for a good marriage, and there seems to be plenty of "magic" in the mix.

If you scored no lower than 80 to 89 points on one, two, or even all three scales, your risk is still low—and your chances of a successful marriage are *good*.

An example: Suppose your personal compatibility profile adds up to 85, your partner's is 92, and the combination comes out to 88. Your overall Compatibility Quotient might be described this way:

Your partner is a very low-risk candidate for marriage problems. You're at somewhat higher risk, but you're still well within the safe range. And your combination score is also relatively low.

Consequently, your overall CQ suggests that marriage may be appropriate, though it's advisable to confront any problem areas you've identified right now and try to correct them. For example, if one of you has a drug or alcohol problem, significant steps should be taken to correct that risk. As we proceed through this book, we'll be making specific suggestions about how you can improve your CQ and your risk profile.

Scores lower than 80 suggest considerably more serious marital risk. In particular, a result of 70 to 79 points on just one of the three scales indicates that you face an unacceptable degree of danger in any relationship. As a result, you should think long and hard before you enter into a serious or permanent commitment at this time.

If you're already married and your scores are in the 70 to 79 point range on any one of the scales, your Compatibility Quotient also suggests impending danger. It's imperative that you take significant steps to improve your compatibility with your mate on that low profile.

A 70 to 79 reading on two or three of the scales indicates considerably greater risk and increasing cause for concern. You may be able to correct many of your problems with concerted individual effort. But you will want to seek professional help, especially if you seem to be stuck at an impasse or if you're involved in a marriage that's clearly in trouble.

A CQ of less than 70 points on even one of the three scales represents the highest level of risk. If you hope to get married—or if you want your current marriage to succeed—you are almost certainly going to need professional counseling.

Suppose, for instance, that your own personal compatibility profile is below 70. In that case, you should regard yourself as not currently ready to get married. What should you do?

As we've indicated, you're probably going to need to see a professional therapist. In addition, you should try to identify your problem areas by looking back over your CQ calculations. Note those items on which you scored especially high. Then, keep these personal deficiencies in mind as you continue reading with an eye to improving your compatibility wherever possible.

If you already are married and have a personal score below 70, you need to pay special attention to correcting your negative traits and habits. Among other things, your personal profile may have revealed that you are subject to violent fits of anger and have even hit those close to you. If that's the case, the first order of business in your life should be to understand and control your temper.

If your partner's profile is below 70 and you're unmarried, it probably will be best to look elsewhere for a mate. On the other hand, if you're already married to this person, there's still hope, provided you can learn to understand, accept and work with your spouse. We've witnessed a number of successful marital turnarounds, for instance, when one spouse encourages another to seek professional help for chronic despair and depression.

There are, indeed, ways to help a partner raise his or her Compatibility Quotient, as we'll see in our upcoming discussions of different personality types and relationships. Many times, achieving compatibility against significant odds can actually produce a stronger relationship. But make no mistake, this takes work!

If your combination CQ is less than 70 points and both your personal profile and that of your partner are higher, the chances are you both are ready for marriage—but not to each other. If you're already married and find yourself in this situation, we would strongly advise you to identify your problem areas, as reflected in the combination profile, then take decisive steps to change them.

So, how exactly can you use, and perhaps even change, your Compatibility Quotient? To begin to understand the nuts and bolts of this process, let's first consider what makes a great marriage, and how divorce can creep up and shatter what seemed to be a solid relationship.

The Making of
A Durable Marriage

What makes for a durable marriage?

There are a number of factors that can influence the stability of a marital relationship. These "Compatibility Factors," as we call them, include such things as the spouses' educational level, family background, income, race, religion, even geographical setting.

The questionnaire that enabled you to compute your Compatibility Quotient in the previous chapter was based on our understanding of these factors from a variety of demographic surveys, scientific studies and clinical observations. Here is a further explanation of the key Compatibility Factors that can have a significant influence on the viability of your marriage.

A Mutual Ability to Deal with Change in a Relationship

Marriage seems to be an arrangement that will continue forever, regardless of the destructive pressures that may endanger it. Individual marriages may fail in numbers greater than ever before, but the institution apparently remains as appealing as ever.

Almost all of us will marry sooner or later, perhaps because we simply can't figure out a better way to meet our need for love, security or companionship. A small minority of people may join the celibate priesthood, be homosexual, live together "without benefit of matrimony," or otherwise experiment with bold and innovative relationships. Some will resolve never to take the vows of marriage, but the vast majority of us will say "I do" nonetheless.

Even though the fact of marriage is a constant, the *shape* of it has changed dramatically over the years—and continues to change today. The reasons we marry or divorce are intimately tied to social, economic and political trends in our local community and broader society. We may think we choose our mates through some sort of magical attraction, but at the same time we expect our marriages to serve us in the real world. The world, however, is constantly changing, with the result that many couples simply can't handle the volatility and flux.

Abe and Helen had known each other since high school, and they came from very similar, traditional backgrounds. Abe was ambitious, with a life plan completely laid out by the time he was fourteen. He expected to graduate with honors from high school, attend a good college, then enter medical school. His career goal: a surgical residency and a booming private practice. Also, he wanted a supportive wife and a large family.

None of these ambitions and expectations had arisen in a vacuum. Abe's father was an internist with a general family practice, and his mother was the office nurse. Active in all the local charities, Mom had served for years as president of the local school board. Furthermore, she had reared six children with great success, and both she and her husband were greatly admired as pillars of the community in the small town where they lived.

Helen, though an only child, also wanted a large family. She thought she might have missed something not having any siblings, and she envied Abe's large, sprawling and seemingly happy family background.

In addition, Helen liked the idea of being a doctor's wife. But she herself wasn't drawn to nursing or any other medical field. Instead, she majored in early education and earned a grade school teacher's certificate. After working for a few years in the first part of their marriage, she left work to start having children.

So far, so good. But after the third child was born, Helen became restless. For one thing, she started feeling tied down. Big families were great in theory, but at this point in her life, she wasn't so sure she wanted any more children. In fact, with the burgeoning household responsibilities that confronted her, she was beginning to wonder if she had too many kids.

Not only that, Helen was feeling stale. She thought she was becoming a less creative, less interesting person, and one antidote for this problem, she decided, might be to return to teaching, at least as a substitute instructor.

Abe didn't take any of these developments very well. He had already begun his private practice and was earning a good living. Still dreaming of a family as large as his own, he wasn't taken with the idea of stopping at three children. His plan was to have at least six and maybe eight; so he argued, "Why not have them all when the two of us are still young?"

More importantly, he felt strongly that their children needed a full-time, stay-at-home mother. "Why have kids if you're not going to be directly involved in nurturing them to adulthood?" he said.

Helen reluctantly agreed to remain home and be a full-time caretaker for their three children, "at least for the time being," she said. But she was adamant about the future size of their family: "No more kids. I can't handle any more and stay sane!"

Abe felt hurt and angry. He simply didn't understand: "After all, we *agreed* to a definite family plan before we ever got married. We talked all this out in detail, and we agreed!"

But either his partner had failed to express her opinions before their wedding, or her opinions had changed over the years. For the first time, Abe saw that he and Helen had somewhat different goals in life. Their values and expectations may have seemed to coincide during their courtship, but there had been no guarantee that they would remain static over the years.

When Helen finally announced about a year later that she would be enrolling in graduate school, Abe's mostly silent resentment bubbled up into outright anger. "How can you do this?" he said. "How can you abandon me and your children?"

Helen responded that she wasn't abandoning anyone; she just intended to spend more time on herself and less on her children and husband. "That way, I think that in the long run I'll be able to become a better mother and wife," she told him.

They couldn't reach an agreement on their respective desires and plans. Abe made thinly disguised threats about not paying for her education. Helen, for her part, often refused to attend medical functions with Abe, or she showed a decided lack of interest when he brought up concerns and challenges he faced at the hospital.

This couple fought for about two years; then they lapsed into long, ominous silences with each other; finally, they entered into divorce proceedings.

What was going on inside of this husband and wife during their long periods of turmoil? Helen felt perpetually guilty because she still sensed, down deep, that she should be staying at home, caring for her children and being a supportive wife to her husband.

Abe was frustrated and angry a great deal of the time, but perhaps his dominant feeling was confusion. He simply couldn't understand what had happened. Helen was driving him crazy with her changing attitudes toward marriage, but he had never fallen out of love with her. Yet increasingly, he was becoming disappointed with their relationship. Professionally, his life was on course; domestically, things hadn't worked out at all as he had planned.

What Abe really wanted was the kind of marriage and family

life that his own family had enjoyed. Yet he had failed to anticipate that the times and the attitudes of women in our society
might change. He wasn't flexible enough to modify his own expectations and work with Helen to achieve hers.

Helen had originally wanted a traditional domestic life similar to
what Abe had experienced, but she had been vague in her understanding of what it would take to become the happy, satisfied mother
of a large family. Moreover, she had been completely unaware of
how powerfully she might feel the tug of a career and other outside
interests as a means to realize her own personal identity.

In short, this couple ran into trouble with a number of the considerations that we relied on to design the Compatibility Quotient.
You'll recall that achieving compatibility becomes more difficult
under these circumstances:

- when one partner comes from a large family and the other
  is an only child
- when the partners have difficulty compromising and arriv-
  ing at joint family decisions
- when the partners have a hard time talking about sensitive
  issues or avoid them altogether
- when there is disagreement over the number of children you
  want to have
- when one spouse is a full-time student

Each of these considerations applied to the relationship between
Abe and Helen. Unfortunately, neither seemed willing or able to
take steps to become more compatible. As a result, they moved
ahead with their divorce.

In this situation, by the way, it would be too simplistic to say
that the main issue dividing Abe and Helen was women's liberation. To be sure, the increasing opportunities for women in the
workplace have raised their aspirations. But the deeper problem
is that with fast-moving changes in our society, marriage is harder
for everyone today, whether the woman aspires to work outside
the home or not.

COMPATIBILITY FACTOR 2:

A Mutual Acceptance of a Particular Style of Marriage

Too often in a marriage, one spouse will assume that the relationship should operate in one way, while the other spouse believes it's going to operate in a completely different way. For example, the man may think he's going to be the "head of the house" as his father was, but his wife may expect things to be more equal.

To achieve compatibility, spouses must avoid going their separate domestic ways; they must accept *one* common style of marriage. Yet this goal may not be as easy as it first seems.

To understand how to identify different marriage styles, and make constructive efforts toward reconciling clashing attitudes of the husband and wife, it's helpful to delve into a little bit of history. In general, the history of marriage in the Western world can be divided into four stages, according to the noted sociologist John Scanzoni. These stages may be characterized in turn by certain dominant styles or themes:

Style 1: In ancient times, the wife was mostly regarded as a piece of property. The husband had little obligation to her, other than to keep her alive. Her status was only a cut above that of the man's pigs and cows. Wives had practically no formal rights and little or no capacity for independent action.

To be sure, there were exceptions to this dire situation among certain ruling family groups and in some societies that departed from the norm. But overall, the state of women up to the beginning of the eighteenth century was subordinate and servile.

Do Style 1 marriages still exist today? Only in sick, pathological relationships, as where the wife has a disturbed need to be dominated or abused by a man.

Style 2: In the nineteenth century, marriage had evolved into what Scanzoni calls the "head-complement" relationship. The husband is still the head honcho, but the wife isn't just a groveling servant. Her main role is to make him shine. As more than a mere piece of property now, she has the right to expect some degree of emotional as well as physical fulfillment from her man.

But if any sort of impasse develops in the relationship, the wife's duty is still to submit; her "feminine virtue" is measured by the grace she shows in submitting. In the previous century, it was rare for a woman to run about independently in society, following her own ambitions and whims; it was even rarer for her to run *out* of a marriage relationship.

Unlike the situation with Style 1, you can look around and see plenty of legitimate Style 2 relationships today. They may not represent the majority of marriages—and they may not seem particularly fair or desirable to feminists. But these relationships can be quite stable and satisfying if both partners are in agreement that this is what they want.

In the style of the nineteenth-century wife, there are many women who are prepared to be "number two" in the marriage relationship. The army wife, the politician's wife and the corporate executive's wife are common examples. This type of woman is eager to devote her life to advancing her husband's career. Her main goal is to help her husband get ahead by charming his bosses and coworkers, entertaining or doing volunteer work that reflects well on him.

A variant on this theme is the marriage where the woman is the "power behind the throne." In this arrangement, the wife is really the brains of the outfit, but the husband still gets first billing. She may run things, but he's got to get all the credit.

But these nineteenth-century marriage models represent only one possibility in the contemporary world, as is evident in the next two styles of marriage that have emerged in the twentieth century.

Style 3: The current century brought universal suffrage and a host of other gains in women's power and prestige. The typical marital arrangement became one of "senior partner–junior partner." Wives may not have held much stock in the company, but now they sat on its board of directors.

This kind of marriage continues in full force today, where the husband usually earns more than the wife and has the last say in important decisions, such as moving or major purchases. However, the wife often holds down a full-time job, may have significant career aspirations and certainly feels free to speak her mind on the big family issues.

Style 4: Marriages began to move toward true equality of spouses during the Second World War, when for the first time, the economy could not function without the labor of women. Men went off to war in large numbers, and women were left behind to do the work. "Rosie the Riveter" became a fixture in American life. Even when the men returned and displaced many of these "Rosies," the women found they had gained permanent access to jobs that previously had been unavailable to them.

Women's evolving parity came neither from legislation nor from enlightenment. It was mainly an economic issue. For the first time in history, women had independent access to the developing factory and business systems. Also, for the first time wives could contemplate going it alone. They could support themselves, without the help of their men, and this possibility of economic independence increased their power in the family enormously.

With these developments, the newest type of marital relationship emerged, what Scanzoni has identified as one of equal partners. This doesn't mean that women have yet achieved complete equality, but the potential for equality is there.

What has been the impact of these developments on the husband? As more and more economic opportunities are made available to women, husbands are no longer necessarily the chief providers in the family. In fact, the wife may earn as much as or more than her husband.

In some cases, the spouses in an equal marriage may choose to cooperate fully and smoothly in an effort to get their marriage to work. Too often, though, they get involved in competition with each other, or one partner becomes resentful when the other isn't available to fulfill certain needs.

Role interchangeability is probably the major distinguishing feature of this latest form of marriage. There are limits, of course, depending on the drive and motivation of the individual and the openness of particular employers to female workers. But theoretically, there is nothing that men can do that women can't do.

What was unthinkable in the marketplace yesterday is com-

monplace today: Wives may become major breadwinners as lawyers, doctors, firefighters or cops. Husbands, on the other hand,
may become "househusbands" or "Mr. Moms." Sexual freedom is
something both partners are entitled to, in equal measure. It's not
uncommon for equality to be asserted well before marriage vows
are even considered, as when both the man and woman agree that
a date will be Dutch treat.

In the classic model of the equal marriage, the husband and
wife earn comparable salaries, and they respect each other's career
aspirations. Both contribute significantly to the household responsibilities and child rearing. In family decision making, they have
gravitated toward distinct areas of responsibility, where one spouse
defers to the judgment of the other.

Sometimes, of course, this sort of natural leadership isn't possible, as when both husband and wife have a deep interest in a
particular issue like the family vacation plans. In these circumstances, the ideal equal-marriage couple is capable of talking
things out and reaching a suitable compromise.

Needless to say, achieving this marriage model is a tall order.
Recent studies have shown, for instance, that even where both
husband and wife work full time—including situations where they
both pursue extremely demanding, high-powered careers—the wife
still shoulders the large majority of household and child-rearing
duties. As a result, she often feels exhausted, unappreciated and
unfairly used.

Another variant on this equality theme is the relatively rare situation where one of the spouses works to provide a family income
so that the other spouse can pursue causes or interests that bring
in little or no money. In every marriage of this type, *both* spouses
must agree on the overriding importance of the activity that isn't
producing income.

For example, a husband may be the primary breadwinner, while
the wife devotes large amounts of time to establishing a Sunday
school or pursuing other church work. Both acknowledge that
what the wife is doing is more important in terms of transforming
lives and benefiting the community than what the husband is do-

ing. Both are equally committed to the nonprofit cause. Yet each also recognizes that the family support must come from one of the spouses—and the husband may be the most likely candidate.

Another illustration of the cause-oriented, equality-based contemporary marriage is the spouse who works so that the other spouse can follow some artistic commitment. A wife, for instance, may hold down a regular job to enable her husband to be an unpaid or low-paid painter or writer. If both are equally committed to the importance of this artistic calling, there may be a possibility for stability, even when the wife is working and the husband is not.

Although not every marriage these days falls into one of the equal-marriage categories, the shape and stability of all marriages have been affected by the possibility of equality. For women, the potential for equality has ushered in an era of greater choices and options in their relationships with men. With these choices and options has come the greater likelihood of divorce.

COMPATIBILITY FACTOR 3:
The Degree to Which the Partners Accept Divorce as an Option

There's a simple rule of thumb that we've learned to follow in our counseling: If one or both partners in a relationship assume that divorce is a ready option when things begin to go wrong, the outlook for that relationship is relatively dim. Unfortunately, however, divorce as a means to resolve incompatibilities in a relationship has been gaining power and popularity in recent years.

Although the United States has the highest divorce rate in the world, it hasn't always been this way. Marriage in this country, as recently as three or four decades ago, represented permanence, duty and fidelity.

To be married meant to make perhaps the deepest human commitment possible for the sake of the family and for society. Divorce was unacceptable, and it was widely believed that there was spiritual goodness and virtue even in an intolerable marriage. Being married was, in short, for keeps.

Today, however, divorce is no longer a big deal (at least not until people actually get involved in it!). The trends in divorce law reflect our more accepting approach. People may now end a marriage by mutual consent, without fault and without so much as stating a reason.

Even the Roman Catholic church has gone along with the trend, and no longer automatically ostracizes its divorced and remarried members. Instead, church annulments are often easy to obtain.

The parishes in some religious traditions even announce marital separations as part of the Sunday service. Others have actually suggested a church-sanctioned divorce ceremony.

It's hard for many of us to recall the enormous personal stigma that was attached to divorce or to single parenthood as recently as a generation ago. Now we permit people to end unsatisfactory relationships with a minimum of social shame. At the same time, we provide little support for couples who want to stick it out and try to make their marriages work.

The independent earning potential of women has played a big role in the increased acceptance of divorce, in part because female economic power has been translated into bargaining power in relationships. Fewer women feel they must stay locked in a loveless or abusive marriage simply to avoid starvation. Divorce has become a viable alternative since it's now quite possible for a wife to separate from her husband and make it on her own economically.

The implications of female independence for divorce go far beyond simple questions of money, however. For one thing, without clearly defined duties, everything in a marriage, with the possible exception of childbearing, becomes negotiable. Couples can decide for themselves who goes to work, who cares for the kids, who determines where to live, and who chooses what to buy.

In short, there are no fixed rights or inherent sources of authority. The only rules are those that each couple can agree upon. In the last analysis, if they don't agree, they can just get a divorce.

The rapid shift in gender roles that has resulted from greater equality of spouses has caused an unusual level of tension in many marriages—most of the tension often seems to focus on the male in the relationship.

After five or ten thousand years in the driver's seat, many men, even those who are well meaning, may elect to take advantage of the women in their lives. Some may accept the increased income, freer sexuality and other benefits, then refuse to take on their share of domestic responsibilities.

Other men may react another way: Feeling threatened, they may rebel at the broad feminine assault on their traditional power and authority by forsaking wives who become aggressive in asserting their equality and by seeking out women who are more traditional and docile.

Whatever direction a given relationship takes, there is often one overriding constant: Without fixed rules, most marriages have been destabilized. The old "Me Tarzan, you Jane" approach left little doubt about where the man and woman stood. Nowadays, the thrust toward equality of the sexes has left everything up for grabs.

As a by-product of the movement toward equality, women usually feel they have a right to ask for a divorce if things aren't going the way they would like. Similarly, men feel that they have a right to push for a divorce if their spouse isn't measuring up in some way. The virtually untrammeled option of initiating a divorce by the man or the woman has, in effect, become the primary expression of equality in the relationship.

In our experience, most people still enter marriage with the idea that the relationship will last. On the other hand, when difficult problems begin to emerge between a husband and a wife, these same people are often quite willing to turn to divorce as a ready option. There's simply less of an inclination these days to "tough it out" than there was in the past, and the ease of divorce has further eroded the resolve to build longer-lasting relationships.

COMPATIBILITY FACTOR 4:

A Willingness to Subordinate Your Individual Interests to the Joint Interests of the Marriage

The emphasis on individualism, so characteristic of the American way of life, has placed the needs of each person over the welfare of the group to which that person belongs. Each has the right and the responsibility to pursue the satisfaction of his or her needs, regardless of the grief this attitude may cause others.

Furthermore, modern marriage is based on a belief in the relatively unrestricted freedom to satisfy one's individual needs. Yet such a notion assumes that marriage is temporary because, after all, individual needs are always subject to change. The anthropologist Margaret Mead saw the handwriting on the wall as far back as 1949, when she wrote:

> The emphasis on choice carried to its final limits means in marriage, as it does at every other point in American life, that no choice is irrevocable. All persons should be allowed to move if they don't like their present home, change schools, change friends, change political parties, change religious affiliations. With the freedom to choose goes the right to change one's mind. If past mistakes are to be repairable in every other field of human relations, why should marriage be the exception?

The choice of whether or not to remain married has become a matter of individual cost-benefit calculations. When one partner wants out, that's it! No explanations necessary. You may have to settle up with your former spouse financially and make mutual arrangements for the kids. But society says, "It's up to you! There will be no social policy other than self-fulfillment."

Such attitudes are inherently destructive for our society because they encourage less stable families and the development of children who lack proper controls and discipline. The shifting economic and social behavior in today's egalitarian marriages has put enormous pressure on husbands, wives *and* kids.

None of this should be taken to mean that marriage, with all its problems, has become any less important to us. On the other hand, what these trends do suggest is that regardless of the costs to all family members, many spouses just won't tolerate a marriage they find personally unfulfilling.

The dangers of this kind of unrestricted individualism came across clearly and disturbingly in the marriage of Alice and Bruce.

Alice came to see us because their marriage, her second, was failing. She didn't want it to end in divorce, the way her first one had. Yet she readily admitted that unless things changed for the better fairly quickly, she would again be quite willing to resort to divorce because she simply wasn't feeling "fulfilled" in the relationship.

She and Bruce had both been artists when they met, and their strong attraction to one another was enhanced by their mutual talent and sensitivity. After a few years, though, Alice got tired of painting and went back to school to earn a business degree. Upon graduation, she found a lucrative entry-level job on Wall Street, and her career rapidly took off. Soon, she was earning a sky-high income, supplemented by a lavish expense account.

How did Bruce fit into these developments? In Alice's eyes, her husband appeared more and more inadequate, and not at all up to what she felt she deserved in a mate. Even though she had been caught up in a major personal transformation, he hadn't changed at all. He was still content to do nothing but paint. With the shift in her own values toward a greater appreciation of the business life, Alice found she couldn't sit for any time with Bruce before she began to berate him for "not being more ambitious."

As you might expect, Bruce finally walked out. Alice returned from a ten-day business trip to find that he had taken his clothes and other personal possessions and moved in with another woman artist.

Alice called him numerous times and also arranged several "accidental" meetings so that she could beg him to return. His response: "It's just too late."

In short, Bruce wanted nothing more to do with her because he felt she had sold out to materialistic values and, in the process, rejected all that he stood for. He didn't even want a share of their joint assets.

Alice's career has continued to flourish, but she has found herself feeling lonely and unfulfilled. The corporate men she works with "are crashing bores," she says. "All they talk about are mergers and acquisitions and who's going to be paid the most this year." She has dated dozens of these men, but she has never had the slightest interest in trying to establish a permanent relationship with any of them.

At length, Alice met Tyler, a talented actor struggling to make a living. After dating a few weeks, they moved in together and have now been involved in a joint housekeeping arrangement for about four months. But strains are already appearing in the relationship.

Alice says she loves Tyler passionately, yet she can't resist her strong urges to put him down for being economically unsuccessful.

"Could history be repeating itself?" she asks, with more than a little insight into her ongoing problems with men. She wants them to be sensitive, artistic and intellectual, but she also wants them to earn at the rate of a top investment banker!

Tyler, not fully understanding the pattern that Alice tends to fall into with men, thinks it's "cool" that she makes so much money. He's not at all threatened by her earning potential and is quite willing to share and enjoy the largess. Also, he readily relinquishes control over their joint finances to her and encourages her to make all the big domestic decisions.

"After all, she's the expert with money and business, and I'm not," he explains.

But Alice can't get used to the idea that she is the main breadwinner, who also controls the family finances and makes most of the major decisions. The reason that her relationship with Tyler is becoming rather rocky can be traced to several forces that are lowering this couple's Compatibility Quotient:

- Alice's inability to accept her partners for who they were
- Their unbalanced earning potential, with Alice being the dominant breadwinner

- Their divergent value systems
- The short-term nature of their relationship, which has been going on for less than six months
- The fact that they are living together before getting married without bothering to make a complete commitment to one another
- Their apparent inability to talk through and resolve their personal differences

Unless this couple takes immediate, effective steps to improve their compatibility—including the subordination of individualism to the needs of the marriage as a whole—their chances for an enduring marriage are nil. As it stands, if they *do* elect to get married, their relationship is virtually certain to go the way of Alice's marriage to Bruce.

COMPATIBILITY FACTOR 5:
The Age of the Partners

Without question, age is the most important marital compatibility factor that can be derived from demographic studies. Before we get into the specifics of the age issue, let's consider the role of demographic studies and other statistical analyses of marriage.

One approach to the mysteries of marriage is to look closely at broad trends and population characteristics and to infer certain principles from those observations. On one level, the statistical approach may seem neat, scientific and convincing. But the major drawback is that while statistics may apply to large groups, they don't necessarily apply to a particular individual.

For example, you may read that a certain contraceptive has a one percent chance of failure. But if *you* are in the one percent to get pregnant, you aren't going to care if 99 percent of the other users stay safe! Statistics, then, may tell you that your relative risk is small, but they can't assure you that you won't be in that small minority that gets into trouble.

A second problem with statistics is the question of how to apply them practically in your marriage. If you learn, for instance, that in your particular city accountants divorce more frequently than lawyers, do you avoid marrying a CPA and search instead for an attorney?

Or suppose you find that your risks of divorce are greater when you marry someone of a different race or social background. Does this mean you should automatically reject prospective spouses who fall into these categories—even if you fall deeply in love with one of them?

Of course, such rigid reliance on statistics would be silly. But despite the limitations that accompany statistics and demographics, the findings of these disciplines can be helpful as you evaluate the overall risks of a relationship. If you see that many of the statistics and other factors are against you, it probably would be wise to reconsider a permanent commitment.

Now, in this context, let's turn to the question of age. The best known statistical fact is that marrying too young is dangerous. No mere myth, the folk wisdom that you ought to wait if you're younger than twenty is borne out by practically every study:

- Teens are twice as likely to split up as those who marry in their twenties; the divorce rate is even higher when teenage spouses become teenage parents.
- Men who marry in their teens are at least twice as likely to divorce as men who marry in their twenties.
- Women who marry at ages fourteen to seventeen are twice as likely to divorce as women who marry at ages eighteen or nineteen. Furthermore, the younger women are three times as likely to divorce as women married at ages twenty to twenty-four.
- Women who marry at age eighteen or nineteen have failure rates 50 percent greater than those in their twenties.

Except under extraordinary circumstances, then, no one should marry before age twenty. If you're seventeen and force yourself to wait three years, one of two things will probably happen.

First of all, you and your intended may drift apart—an excellent sign that "it was never meant to be." Or your relationship may endure and you'll marry with a much better chance of success. Brains and good looks are simply not enough. There is no question that a modicum of maturity is essential to sustain a marriage, and that usually means aging into your twenties.

On the other hand, when people marry beyond their twenties, the divorce rate begins to rise again, albeit slightly. The increase seems to affect women more than men—that is, older women are more likely to get divorced than older men.

Why are older people more at risk than those in their twenties? The studies haven't definitively revealed a cause, but many experts feel that older people are more loathe to give up their independence, less accustomed to sharing a bed and, in general, more set in their ways.

If you and your fiancé happen to be in your twenties, it's important not to become complacent. A reliance just on one set of statistics, such as those relating to the age factor, can be misleading.

Consider, for instance, the fact that the average age at first marriage has been rising steadily into the twenties for the last fifty years. Specifically, in the past decade the average man who married for the first time was twenty-six, and the average woman's age was twenty-four.

From these trends, you might expect that increasingly older marriages would lower the overall divorce rate. As we all know, however, this hasn't been the case. Perhaps the current rate of marriage failure would be even greater than 50 percent if the average age of first marriages had remained low.

COMPATIBILITY FACTOR 6:

Getting to Know Your Partner before Marriage

Courtship may be an old-fashioned idea, but it's also a good idea. Up to a point, the longer the length of acquaintance before marriage, the stronger the chance for marital success. The reasons are fairly obvious: After all, the more you get to know each other, the better your chances will be of figuring out whether you can tolerate one another's quirks.

Oddly enough, however, sexual compatibility, which many people assume should be a component of "getting to know" a partner, is probably the least important factor. Good sex is usually the result of two people getting along, not the other way around.

Couples frequently complain that their sex life was excellent when they lived together, but that it plummeted after they got married. Why is this?

In many cases, sexual pleasure blooms in the first few months of a relationship because of the newness and freshness of the experience. When sex is involved before the couple is married, there are few of the concerns that accompany a long-term commitment, such as intricate organizing of family finances or planning for children. As a relationship ages, however, the importance of the sexual experience typically recedes and other concerns come to the fore.

In the last analysis, there's certainly no reason for sex to become an unpleasant or unimportant part of the relationship after marriage. But that's exactly what may happen if the couple fails to prepare for the nonsexual challenges and decisions that every long-term relationship requires.

Engagements are important for learning how two people function together in a variety of situations. Just about anyone can get along during the first heady days or even months of infatuation. But how about afterwards?

When the months begin to approach a year or more, the partners must focus on whether they have the same tastes in friends, leisure activities, music or travel. They begin to see whether they can really tolerate each other's parents. They find out whether or not they like to relax in the same way. When they disagree, they have a better idea about how easy or hard it is for the two of them to resolve their differences.

To give a couple time to see if their relationship can be successfully turned into a marriage, we recommend a courtship period of at least six months, preferably twelve months, and in some cases as long as two years.

On the other hand, too much of a good thing can be counter-productive. Very lengthy courtships—those over three or four years, for example—are associated with high rates of divorce.

We believe that a year or two is generally enough to decide. People who take longer are probably unsure that they really want to make a permanent commitment. They may finally do so, but in many cases, these foot draggers haven't really completely made up their minds.

Consequently, we give courtships of less than six months or more than three years low marks on the Compatibility Quotient. Those in the six-month to three-year range are more desirable. But keep in mind that 1989 University of Wisconsin study we cited in the first chapter: No matter how long you've gone out with a person, actually living together beforehand seems to work against a marriage.

COMPATIBILITY FACTOR 7:

The Tradition of Divorce in Your Family

There's some statistical validity to the notion that divorce runs in families.

For one thing, a number of studies have reported a consistent trend for children of divorced parents to end up divorced themselves. Grown children from divorced families have a 50 percent greater chance of getting divorced than grown children from intact families. Conversely, children of long-married parents tend to have high Compatibility Quotients.

There are three possible theories that have been offered to explain the importance of the stability or instability of the parental marriages of each partner in a relationship. These are the role model theory, the economic theory, and the parental guidance theory.

THE ROLE MODEL THEORY.

This concept states that divorced parents have demonstrated by their actions that separation is an acceptable solution to marital unhappiness.

It's well known that parents teach their children by example, whether positive or negative. No matter how hard the child may try to avoid it, he or she often ends up doing just what his or her parents did many years ago.

Adult children of alcoholic parents, for instance, often turn out to be alcoholic, even if they swore to themselves that they would never succumb. Similarly, victims of child abuse are the very individuals who end up beating their own kids. Even if we've hated our experiences, we seem to learn more from what we've been exposed to in the real world than from any other source.

Divorce is also a learned behavior. Some couples will stick it out, no matter what. Divorce is simply not a possibility. Perhaps dissolving the tie is unacceptable for religious reasons, or because of strong personal convictions which have nothing to do with religion. The role model theory, then, holds that individuals are more likely to accept divorce if they have been exposed to it in their own families.

THE ECONOMIC THEORY.

This idea maintains that parental divorce is usually accompanied by downward social mobility for the entire family. The decline in turn breeds marital instability in the offspring. In other words, after parents divorce there may be less money. Children then may marry young to escape their poverty; or they may cut their education short; or they may take other unwise steps that place them at higher risk for divorce.

THE PARENTAL GUIDANCE THEORY.

This explanation for the tendency of parental divorce to influence divorce among children states that divorcing parents are often inattentive to their offspring. They may become too preoccupied with survival issues to be able to provide adequate parental supervision. As a result, the children, being without proper training or guidance in their human relationships, may be inclined to make a poor choice of mate. Divorce is a consuming process, and divorcing parents are likely to be wrapped up in their own problems for extended periods of time. The cycle of divorce thus perpetuates itself.

How can you protect yourself if you come from a family with an experience of divorce?

We suggest that you stay particularly alert to your extra vulnerability for divorce, especially if your potential husband or wife is also from a divorced family. If you find yourself in marital trouble, ask yourself, "Am I blindly following a script laid out by Mom and Dad?"

Then, discuss the problem of your parent's divorce frankly and openly with your partner. Acknowledge that your background puts you in a higher risk category for divorce. Finally, enlist your partner's aid to prevent your marriage from falling into the same traps faced by your parents.

COMPATIBILITY FACTOR 8:

The Strength of Your Social Support System

Couples who are part of a solid social network have higher Compatibility Quotients than those who live in isolation. For example, divorce rates tend to be lower where there is a strong involvement with a stable extended family or with a tightly knit community. Regular church attendance—though not necessarily religious belief—is correlated with a low divorce rate.

According to some couples we've worked with, the deep involvement in a church community, especially one where divorce is frowned upon, makes it extremely uncomfortable for a couple to separate. The pressure of the religious community encourages marital partners to try their hardest to work things out before they split.

In contrast, the CQ is relatively low for couples without community or family support systems in a transient atmosphere, such as a sprawling singles apartment complex or an impersonal metropolis. This is not to say that those who live in apartment complexes or cities can't keep their marriages together, but they should be aware that their living situation may put a higher level of stress on their marriage.

We typically advise those in big-city situations to try to break down the metropolis into a warmer, more manageable community. One of the best ways to do this is to join a church or synagogue, or otherwise link up with stable family networks.

COMPATIBILITY FACTOR 9:

Your Geographical Area

"Go east, young man" is our advice. But stay away from the big cities.

It's long been observed that rates of divorce increase as one moves from the Northeast to the Southwest section of the United States. In 1981, for example, the divorce rate for the Southwest was 75 percent higher than for the Northeast.

A number of reasons have been proposed to explain this phenomenon, none of which strike us as completely satisfactory. Some argue that there may be more dislocations and adjustments that easterners must face in moving westward. Others say that in the smaller cities and towns of the Northeast there are more deeply rooted traditions that enhance family stability. The western sections of the country, in contrast, are newer, more transient and in a state of greater flux. Whatever the reasons, the Northeast currently gets the nod for marital stability.

On the other hand, divorce rates are high for almost all major cities throughout the nation, whether in the West, South or East. At the same time, divorce is less common in smaller towns and suburbs; the divorce rate is even lower in rural areas.

Among cities, the Sunbelt in particular seems to the the "divorce belt." If you have a choice—and we recognize that most people don't—remember that living in a city *and* in the South or West can give your Compatibility Quotient a double negative jolt. But if you want to enhance your chances for marital stability, the best advice might be "Go live on a farm in Massachusetts!"

COMPATIBILITY FACTOR 10:

Commitment to a Cause

Two people may share a commitment to some ideal greater than their marriage, and at least for a time, this cause may help them transcend many of the problems that might otherwise endanger their relationship.

Peggy and Frank, a middle-aged couple who recently came to us for marital help, illustrate this sort of relationship. On one level, this couple had always seemed to get along quite well. They both had a similar sense of humor; they liked to make small talk about the same things; and they both enjoyed the same kinds of movies, plays and music concerts. From most outward appearances, Peggy and Frank appeared to have a lot going for them. Both were highly responsible people, and they were regarded by all their friends as the most stable couple around.

Unfortunately, though, they rarely engaged in intimate discussions about their deepest personal thoughts and feelings. They stayed together for most of thirty years with few fights and a lot of fun and enjoyment for one major reason—their children. Their two sons and one daughter had become a joint "cause" that had given their relationship meaning and kept them together.

As parents, they had become models of maturity and reliability. They had worked hard to raise three children, and they had succeeded in producing two college graduates and one about ready to leave for school. All seemed well on their way to making a mark in the world.

But now, after thirty years of marriage, with their children gone and no other cause to fill in the gap, they complained there was little communication and no sex.

These were not new problems, by the way. The inherent flaws in their relationship simply had been covered over by the demands of the cause. Peg and Frank had not slept together for at least a year. Furthermore, they had not worked at deepening their interactions with one another, beyond their joint participation in social events or talking about their children.

Their successful careers hadn't helped shore up their relationship, either. Frank was a respected lawyer, and Peggy was a top administrator for the American Cancer Society. Frank had always supported his wife's work because he believed in it, independently of her involvement. Over the years he had volunteered generous amounts of his time and money to the local Cancer Society chapter. But even this common interest hadn't blossomed so as to give their marriage meaning apart from their children.

This couple's relationship now faced a crisis. Peggy became suspicious that her husband was involved with another woman since he didn't seem interested in sex with her. In fact, Frank wasn't engaged in an affair, nor was he sexually inadequate. Like his wife, he had just fallen into the habit of not engaging in sex.

Frank didn't want the marriage to break up, but he knew that the relationship was empty, and he was tired of the suspicion that had been directed toward him. As for Peggy, she also wanted to stay together, but she was confused because all the meaning now seemed to have gone out of her life with the departure of her children.

What should this couple do?

Our advice went like this: They should first recognize that they had been relying on a cause, their children, to impart meaning to their relationship. There's nothing wrong with affirming such a worthy joint cause. But the danger is that by itself, almost any cause, even one that seems eternal, will eventually play itself out. Even an ongoing religious, political or social commitment can eventually change direction. With this change, the marriage relationship must fall back on itself, on the personal resources of the spouses, apart from any outside help.

In this case, we helped this couple rebuild its sexual relationship—something the partners both wanted but didn't quite know how to do. They began to experience some romance again, as they lingered over dinner at a nice restaurant and then headed for the bedroom when they arrived back home.

Also, we encouraged them to engage in conversations about issues that concerned them alone, such as planning husband-wife vacations and making preparations for their retirement, which was only a few years away.

Finally, we latched onto a natural new cause for them to pursue: the Cancer Society. We encouraged Frank to intensify his involvement in volunteer activities with patients, and we also suggested that Peggy help him more in pursuing these activities. After all, as one of the Society's executives, she was the expert.

These suggestions were all this couple needed to begin to put their marriage back together again. Clearly, a cause by itself may not be able to keep a marriage together—and in fact, it may even obscure important, festering issues the couple should confront. But properly employed, a joint cause can enhance the deeper meaning of any relationship.

COMPATIBILITY FACTOR 11:
The Company You Keep

Misery loves company, but so does marital happiness. There are no better salespeople for marriage than happily married men and women. They are often the ones who "fix up" their unattached friends and relatives, usually in a sincere attempt to spread their contentment.

Divorced people, on the other hand, may be down on marriage. In many cases, when the divorce is relatively recent, they are bitter and cynical, and perhaps they have a right to be. But there is serious danger in their excessive references to their former spouses, or their advice to be wary about the motives of the opposite sex.

Generally speaking, it's hard for one person to ruin another's happy marriage. But a disgruntled refugee from a broken relationship can put a lot of pressure on a marriage that is already weak.

Loose talk among those with a history of marital problems can actually help trigger divorce epidemics in a neighborhood or town. In one suburban neighborhood, for instance, Mary Jo had just been deserted by her husband, and her discussions on the subject of male unreliability caused Betty Jean to wonder if she should also leave her husband.

A few houses down the street, Hank was openly cheating on his wife. Both Betty Jean and Mary Jo knew about Hank's unfaithfulness, and his antics just fueled their negative attitudes toward marriage and men. Not only that, Hank introduced his good friend, Larry, who was feeling restless in his own marriage, to his lover's sister. It became known around the neighborhood that Hank and Larry were often double-dating (and double-cheating).

The upshot of these complex shenanigans was that all four of these people—Betty Jean, Mary Jo, Hank and Larry—ended up getting divorced. We didn't trace which other marriages may have been affected by this particular social virus, but I'm sure the devastation wasn't limited to these four couples.

We all like to believe we are independent thinkers. But the fact is that whether we like it or not, we are heavily influenced by the people with whom we associate. It would be wise for you and your partner to examine your outside contacts and relationships. If you find that you have a preponderance of divorced friends and very few married ones, you're certainly exposing your own marriage to some risk. Some readjustment of your network of friendships may be in order.

The idea here is not to avoid your divorced friends or those who are having marital difficulties. Just be sure that they're not the only person with whom you associate.

To this end, we suggest that you follow what we call the "one-third, two-thirds rule." This approach involves organizing your social contacts so that at least two-thirds of your encounters with other people will involve situations, attitudes and individuals having a positive impact on your marriage. The other one-third of your interactions may include those people with marital difficulties. This way, you'll be exposed to a much heavier dose of uplifting influences, rather than to those forces that pull your marriage down.

COMPATIBILITY FACTOR 12:

The Spouses' Occupations

Numerous studies have tried to identify those occupations or professions that breed heavy divorce rates, but results have been contradictory and confusing. One generally consistent finding, however, is that people with occupations providing high status and high income tend to have lower divorce rates than their low-status, low-income counterparts.

Still, it's hard to generalize from such findings because there are so many exceptions, especially among the very famous or the very wealthy. You only have to pick up your daily newspaper or weekly newsmagazine and turn to the gossip, entertainment or "people in the news" sections to be overwhelmed by the divorces, infidelities and other troubles that afflict well-off celebrities.

Some data suggest that the actual work itself may exert a less important impact on the marriage than the conditions of the work. For example, high divorce rates are associated with jobs that have long or irregular hours, frequent travel, close contact with workers of the opposite sex, or easy opportunities to consume alcohol.

Job satisfaction and the level of job stress are two other influential factors. Contented employees often make contented mates. Also, the tendency to transfer work frustrations onto the spouse or family is common.

To maximize the Compatibility Quotient in the occupational area, then, an unmarried person might try to pick a spouse who likes his or her job, who works regular hours, who gains sufficient prestige and income from the job, who seems to manage the stresses and pressures of work fairly well, and whose work doesn't require out-of-town trips with members of the opposite sex.

If you're married and either you or your spouse has a job that threatens the stability of your marriage, you may find it difficult to change your style of work. After all, the basic demands of the job may be such that the only way you can change is to quit. If you have a family to support, that option may not seem too attractive.

Most jobs are subject to some degree of change and adjustment. One attorney, for instance, found that the hours he spent at the office had been getting longer and longer. He regularly began to get home after 9:00 P.M. on weekdays, when his two young children already had been tucked into bed. Also, he had fallen into a pattern of working on Saturdays.

Finally, although he generally liked his work, the long hours had taken a toll in imposing more stress on him than he could comfortably handle. He simply needed more free time to unwind, relax and prepare for the next series of challenges at the office.

This lawyer's wife was holding down a demanding job as a corporate executive, and she felt she was having to carry too much of the load for managing the household and rearing the children. Also, neither she nor the two youngsters got to see much of Dad.

The solution this couple reached was initially nerve-racking for the husband. After a series of difficult but constructive conversations with his wife, he agreed that he needed to spend more time at home. Then came the hard part: He had to raise this issue with the senior partner who was his supervisor.

"I can just see my career going down in flames when I bring this up to him," he moaned.

But in fact, the senior partner agreed with the younger attorney's analysis of his problem, and together they mapped out a plan that allowed the junior lawyer to spend more time at home. As a result, this man's position as a lawyer didn't suffer, and his position as a husband and father was greatly strengthened.

COMPATIBILITY FACTOR 13:

Educational Levels

The educational level of the spouses is often positively correlated with marital stability. Specifically, men and women with less than a high school diploma have especially high rates of divorce, and those with college degrees have relatively low rates.

The link between education and marital longevity is probably partly rooted in income considerations. Those with higher educational levels on average make higher incomes; higher incomes are associated with longer-lasting relationships.

But economics isn't the only connection between modest education and higher divorce rates. People who drop out of high school are probably less persistent than those who complete their education. Persistence, as a trait that helps one overcome the frustrations of school, may also promote a greater ability to cope with the inevitable frustrations of marriage.

Furthermore, a man with less education than either of his parents is an increased risk for divorce. Again, the reasons for this aren't entirely clear. One possibility is that those with highly educated parents tend to have high aspirations. These same offspring may, in turn, become frustrated if they lack the skills and knowledge to realize their aspirations. Their frustration may spill over into other areas of their life and finally taint their marriage.

Too much schooling, however, does not always help in keeping marriages together. Statistics reveal that women with long years of postgraduate education have much more marital instability than those who stopped right after college. Probably these perennial students have less of a commitment to marriage than to career or academic pursuits, and so they're more prone to turn to divorce if the relationship begins to run into trouble.

To sum up: If you select a spouse who has little schooling, you're going to jeopardize your Compatibility Quotient. On the other hand, if you're a man whose wife starts graduate training during the marriage, your risk is also increased. Finally, any changes during the marriage that throw the educational levels of the spouses out of balance may signal danger for the durability of the relationship.

One couple who came to see us was on the brink of divorce, despite having made it through twenty-eight years of marriage. When they first met, the husband had been a carpenter, and the wife was a secretary. Both had only a high school education, and in many ways they had seemed made for each other.

She had been attracted by his shy, gentle manner and his sensitivity. At the same time, she recognized his basic talent, and she quickly became his most ardent supporter and adviser. Among other things, she encouraged him to take college courses that would enhance his career. Finally, he earned his degree.

This woman always encouraged her husband to get ahead, not for her sake but for his own self-esteem. Gradually, he hired a few helpers and began to build houses on his own. With his wife's support, his business grew, and eventually he started building whole developments. Today, he controls a multimillion-dollar real estate business.

Needless to say, the husband is no longer the shy little carpenter. He dresses well and talks with self-assurance. His wife seems mousy and poorly educated in comparison. But she has refused to spend money on herself, even though there is more than enough. Also, through the years she resisted taking university courses because, as she said, "I have too much to do around the house."

There has been a price to pay for these changes. Because his wife began to seem drab and unexciting, the husband started to have affairs with other women. He then insisted he wanted out of the marriage because "I'm bored. We've grown in different directions."

The couple finally did get a divorce—not because they had been unsuited for one another when they first married, but because they had failed to develop at the same educational and social pace. A crash college course would never have saved this marriage because the couple had grown too far apart.

To maximize your Compatibility Quotient, educational and career decisions must be thoroughly explored by both partners, and both must be in substantial agreement. If one spouse advances more rapidly than the other, however, that's a major danger signal. The "leading" mate must pause to allow the other to catch up and the "trailing" spouse must take decisive steps to close any educational or social gaps. Otherwise, one mate will indeed outgrow the other, and the marriage will be placed at substantial risk.

COMPATIBILITY FACTOR 14:
The "Mix" of the Marriage

It's difficult enough to make a marriage succeed when both partners come from similar religious, social and ethnic traditions, but the problems compound rapidly when there are marked differences in backgrounds. There are no hard-and-fast rules in this area, except for one: The more dissimilar the two partners are, the lower their Compatibility Quotient will be.

Religious differences can present major problems, even if neither spouse is particularly devout. There are issues of loyalty to your own church and a feeling of alienation from the religious tradition of your mate.

Also, a common question that arises after a marriage has begun is how to raise the children: Should they be Catholic? Or Methodist? Or both?

Finally, problems may arise in interactions with relatives on both sides. It may become quite difficult to visit your partner's parents if your spouse has grown up in a Unitarian tradition that's suspicious of southern evangelicals. On the other side, things can become unpleasant if the Baptist parents always raise the issue of whether you and your children are preserving the family's born-again religious customs.

Mixed race marriages may present even more difficulties. Unlike religion, where conversion is a possibility and where grassroots ecumenical forces are tending to bring those of divergent traditions closer together, neither spouse can change the color of skin. Strong black, white and Asian communities are often less than enthusiastic about embracing racially mixed newlyweds.

In order for a mixed race marriage to have a decent chance, it's essential that the Compatibility Quotient be high in just about every other area. Partners must be extremely compatible to counterbalance the extraordinary stresses that they are bound to face. The marriage will survive only if the two spouses are *fanatically* dedicated to one another.

When race and even religion are the same, there can still be marked differences in ethnic background that may influence the Compatibility Quotient. Italian Catholics, for example, may not feel comfortable with Irish Catholics. [In fact, those of Italian heritage may actually feel more at home with Jews because of greater similarities in their cultures.]

Protestants from different backgrounds also may have very little in common. Episcopalians, for instance, are often quite wary of those from the evangelical and free church traditions, like some members of the Pentecostal and independent Bible churches. They may fear that the free-churchers are too "demonstrative" or too "undignified" in their expressions of faith. The evangelicals, for their part, may feel uncomfortable around Episcopalians and Roman Catholics because of their use of wine in Holy Communion and also their acceptance of social drinking.

Even Methodists and Baptists in certain parts of the South and Southwest may be inherently suspicious and unaccepting of one another. One Methodist from the Fort Worth area in Texas, for instance, found that she was unable to accept her Baptist boyfriend's statements about his religious beliefs at face value. Instead, she constantly looked for the "Baptist connection" in his most innocent comments and observations. Finally, the young man tired of the analysis and criticism and looked elsewhere for a companion.

When all else is equal, serious tensions can still result between two partners from very different backgrounds. Suspicions and resentments that are rooted in diverse family traditions don't simply disappear when two young people fall in love.

So, it's important to take a hard look at who and what you and your partner are—religiously, racially, ethnically and socially. If you are too different in background, and you also seem incompatible in other ways, it's best to part ways before you enter into a marriage. If you're already married and you face these differences, your work will be cut out for you as you attempt to increase your compatibility in those areas where change and adjustment are possible.

These Compatibility Factors, which may exert a significant influence on your CQ, are just the tip of the iceberg in your attempt to determine how well you may get along with your partner. Another equally important set of considerations is the personality type of your spouse or of the person you hope to marry. Let's look at some of the possible "problem partners" you may run into, and explore possible ways of dealing with them.

I I

Problem Partners

FOUR

The Emotional
Roller Coaster

On your first encounter with the Emotional Roller Coaster, you may think, "Life will never be boring if we get married! What a fascinating, stimulating person!"

But think again.

A number of the questions we posed on the Compatibility Quotient suggest that those who become involved with this problem personality may be in for some trying, irritating, exasperating times. Instead of fun and excitement, the Roller Coaster more often offers anger, despair, drunkenness, drug abuse and other uncontrolled expressions of inner turmoil.

This person, who may as easily be a woman as a man, tends to be thoroughly unpredictable and impulsive. He or she often experiences a wide and abrupt range of feelings, from ecstatic happiness one day to deep despair the next. As the name implies, the Roller Coaster's life is usually accompanied by high excitement and sometimes by precarious adventure—though his or her companion may not enjoy going along for the ride.

The Emotional Roller Coaster is highly susceptible to boredom. Things always have to be changing and providing stimulation, or a sense of emptiness and tedium may set in. If there are no outside forces that break through to relieve the sense of boredom, the Roller Coaster often feels compelled to generate some.

Living with a volatile companion frequently means having to put up with violent arguments, self-destructive acts, recurrent accidents, poor planning, and a tendency to inject intense emotional conflict into even the most ordinary daily experiences. In extreme cases, this person may even ponder or attempt suicide.

Although people in this category may display a wide range of feelings and behaviors, their predominant emotion is an anger which masks a deep sense of despair and meaninglessness. They become enraged over trifles, events so small or insignificant that those around them are puzzled and dismayed. Furthermore, there often seems to be no pattern to their fits of anger. The tantrums sweep in like mini-tornadoes on a clear day and leave havoc and devastation among family members who get in the way.

These intensely angry people often try to rationalize their behavior after the fact. If you listen to them carefully, though, you'll find that their rationalizations and justifications don't add up. In many instances, no amount of reasoning and cajoling will prevent their extravagant displays of rage, or otherwise motivate them to achieve a balance between their lows and highs.

Emotional Roller Coasters may offer their companions a great time, at least initially. But as the relationship wears on, disturbing signs begin to appear—as Jack discovered a little too late with Meg.

Meg's Ups And Downs

Meg was a gorgeous young woman, extremely intelligent, bubbly in her conversation and quite talented as a classical pianist. Her mother had died when she was a child, and her well-to-do father was usually on the road. So she and her brother were raised by a never-ending series of housekeepers.

Meg's father never remarried, claiming that he didn't want to bring a new mother into the house and risk upsetting the children. In his way, he was deeply devoted to Meg and her brother and spent a great deal of money on their education and extracurricular activities. Unfortunately, he wasn't at home much, and so the children had to fend for themselves in learning to cope with the world and in developing their own personal values.

Meg's solution was to turn on a bright, cheery, almost manic personality in initial encounters with the girls and especially with the boys she knew. Relying on this veneer of exuberance, she found that she could provoke a favorable, friendly response from many of the girls, and intense sexual interest in the boys.

In the time she spent alone, though, Meg wrestled with serious bouts of despair. At the deepest level, she lacked confidence in herself. She didn't know where her life was going, and she suspected that despite the money her father poured into her life, he didn't really care for her that much. "Otherwise, why wouldn't he spend more time with me?" she reasoned.

The more she thought about her father, the madder she became with him. Yet he was rarely around for her to show him her feelings, and so she learned to bottle them up and try to get on with her life.

At times, Meg even toyed with the idea of suicide. After a series of dates with attractive boys or even after an election to some school position, she didn't feel particularly fulfilled. "Is this all there is to life?" she wondered. It didn't seem that she should be dissatisfied or bored, given her popularity. Yet she was, and that made her even angrier. In fact, in a complex way, her boredom arose as a direct result of the anger she was trying to contain.

Early on, Meg learned that she could divert her attention from her anger and ease those feelings of boredom by provoking exciting events and affecting great exuberance in her relationships with others. So she was the first in her junior high school class to smoke. She was the first to get drunk. She was the first to try marijuana.

She was usually the first to suggest a crazy outing—"Tonight, how about a mixed skinny-dipping party?" And she was by far one of the freest in her physical encounters with the opposite sex.

As Meg grew older, graduated from college and entered the job market, she began to experience some success as a junior executive in a department store chain. Also, she continued to attract plenty of interested men. Yet her struggle with her volatile emotions continued.

She typically fell madly in love on the first date with many of the eligible young men who asked her out. She actually convinced herself on dozens of occasions that "this is the perfect guy." Then, she would plunge into a freewheeling sexual relationship and go out with that particular man every evening for a straight week or two.

Soon, though, the initial excitement and fascination would abate, and she would become bored. Her latent anger would surface, and she would say or do something that would trigger a massive argument. With this clash, the romantic bubble would burst. Meg usually would walk away quaking in rage, and her companion would be left speechless, wondering exactly what he had done wrong.

This pattern of euphoria and crashing failure in her love relationships continued until Meg was in her early thirties, at which point she met Jack. Jack was a divorced father of three who was nearly fifty, but despite their differences, the two quickly fell in love.

After a few weeks, Meg launched one of those self-destructive arguments that had been her trademark in the past. But this time, she received a different response: Jack met her verbal onslaught with calm, soothing words and a refusal to fight. Meg was completely disconcerted; all she could manage to do was attack him once more, then sputter for a few minutes, and finally stomp off toward home.

At the same time, however, Meg became more fascinated than ever by Jack. "Why didn't he get mad at me?" she wondered. "I really abused him, and I know I wasn't being completely fair. Yet he just smiled and took it. What's wrong with him?"

In fact, nothing was wrong with Jack. He was naturally a rather calm, even phlegmatic person, who rarely got excited about anything. It did bother him that Meg had behaved so explosively toward him. But he just decided, "She's got a lot of fire. I could use some more excitement in my life."

This couple continued to date, and against the sound advice of a number of their friends, they got married. Things proceeded rather peacefully for the first year of marriage, largely because Jack ignored Meg's emotional highs and lows. When she was on a "high," he enjoyed the excitement she generated; when she was in the dumps, he usually stayed out of her way until the mood passed.

One thing which bothered Jack more than he let on was Meg's tendency to drink heavily and occasionally to use marijuana and cocaine when she was feeling low. She sometimes seemed unable to manufacture emotional peaks on her own, and in those situations, she increasingly began to fall back on alcohol and drugs.

Jack found that he could put up with most of this behavior, despite the misgivings he had about the substance abuse. But things eventually came to a head when Meg announced that she wanted a child—a subject they had never seriously discussed before marriage.

Jack resisted: "No, I've had enough of kids."

He was still supporting and visiting his three, who ranged from age nine to nineteen and who were still in school.

"But we're talking about *my* children, not the ones you've had by another woman!" she shouted.

This time, though, Jack stood firm. Unaccustomed to such resistance, Meg ran off to her room in tears, locked the door, and refused to come out for dinner that evening. Then, she started throwing things around in the room and even threatened to take an overdose of the sleeping pills she kept in her drawer.

Finally, Jack relented and said he would at least be willing to entertain the idea of having another child. "But we have to sit down and talk about it. I can't think with you yelling through a locked door."

After a couple of lengthy discussions, Jack finally gave in and agreed to have a child. Knowing the strain that children could put on a problem-plagued marriage, however, he insisted that they go in for marital counseling *before* Meg got pregnant. She reluctantly consented to this arrangement, and with the therapist's help, this couple managed to reduce some of the tension they were experiencing in their relationship.

Among other things, Meg, for the first time in her life, began to understand how she was ruled by her need for excitement and her desire to escape the boredom that she so deeply feared. Also, she realized that she harbored deep-rooted hostilities, which could probably be traced back to her relationship with her father.

As for Jack, he learned more about dealing with his own limited ability to express his emotions and with his fears of experiencing a second failed marriage.

Even with professional help, however, this couple continued to face rough times. The arrival of a child imposed additional strains on their relationship, as Jack had feared. At least they are trying hard to deal effectively with their difficulties. They now seem to have a better than even chance of making their relationship work.

What Motivates the Emotional Roller Coaster?

To some extent, Meg was trying to manipulate Jack when she exploded or threatened to hurt herself. She wanted a baby, and she was willing to try almost any means to force him to bend to her wishes.

On the other hand, like other Roller Coasters, Meg was acting out of deep-seated conditioning that was well beyond her personal control. Her swings from happiness to despair to rage weren't in any way a sham; she really felt them. Not only that, she *needed* the emotional ups and downs to make her life reasonably bearable and interesting. Part of the therapy she is now undergoing has been designed to help her understand how her emotions work and to enable her to become less a slave of the radical shifts in her feelings.

There are conflicts and misunderstandings in every relationship, of course, and most of us have learned to deal with them. Usually, we can nurse our bruised feelings, talk out the problems with our partner and then move on.

Not so with Emotional Roller Coasters. Even a mild conflict may cause these men and women to lose control. Without warning or reason, wild laughter or happiness may strike. On the spur of the moment, the Roller Coaster personality may trigger some event designed to create high excitement or emotional stimulation.

A touch of sadness may quickly turn to utter grief among those subject to the Roller Coaster phenomenon. A touch of joy may become unbounded rapture, and anger, unmitigated rage.

This problem personality always has difficulty with intimate relationships that demand an intensity with and commitment to others. The Roller Coaster often doesn't really know who he is—what his basic identity consists of—because his self-image has been fragmented into bits and pieces that have failed to coalesce.

What may seem to be manipulation, as in Meg's case, may actually be a series of desperate attempts at self-preservation. The Roller Coaster must rant and demand and cajole in order to cling to his chosen source of nourishment—to the emotional "fix" he gains from those temporary feelings of euphoria or excitement.

No spouse can provide everything the Roller Coaster needs all the time. Consequently, relationships involving this type of person are usually doomed to failure.

How Can You Identify an Emotional Roller Coaster?

Obviously, there are varying degrees of emotional volatility. Relatively mild swings in mood aren't anything to worry about. In fact, it really *is* more interesting and exciting to be around someone who likes to take reasonable risks, participate in new activities, and in general have a lot of fun.

On the other hand, if one or, even worse, both partners have extremely explosive personalities, with marked movements of feeling and mood, the marriage will be headed for big trouble.

How can you identify and assess the risks of the roller coaster ride you may be facing? First of all, you'll get a good idea of the prospects for compatibility between you and your partner by re-examining your Compatibility Quotient at this time. Look especially closely at those responses that relate to some of the concepts we've been discussing in this chapter.

Ask yourself the following six questions about your partner. Finally, after you've finished, turn the questions around and ask them of yourself.

1. HOW IMPULSIVE IS YOUR PARTNER?

People are often drawn to the Emotional Roller Coaster because they lack excitement in their own lives. When they encounter a person who often acts on impulse, without much thought for the consequences of his or her actions, they think they have found someone who can supplement their own deficiencies in creativity or having fun.

Unfortunately, though, what these unsuspecting people often end up with is a partner who is an emotional child. Initiative and risk taking are quite desirable in some circumstances. So are courage and imagination. But wild impulsiveness will drive most normal people to the edge of patience and inner stability. Just as important, those who are overly impulsive will inevitably undermine the Compatibility Quotient in their love relationships.

To check the level of impulsiveness in your relationship, ask yourself the following questions:

- Does your partner have a reputation for sexual promiscuity?
- Does he or she go on wild shopping sprees?
- Is there a history of binges, such as excessive eating or drinking?
- Has he or she been known to engage on the spur of the moment in exceptionally foolish or even illegal activities, such as attacking someone physically or shoplifting?

Occasional impulsiveness won't significantly affect the Compatibility Quotient, but regular or gross instances of this trait will signal potential trouble.

2. DOES HE OR SHE GET ANGRY WITHOUT APPARENT CAUSE?

Although everyone becomes angry at one time or another, the Emotional Roller Coaster makes it to the boiling point more than most people. Those furious outbursts also are more intense than those of the average person.

The partner who is not the Roller Coaster should ask, "Did I really say or do anything to warrant so much rage?"

If the two of you were cuddling just an hour before, but now your partner seems to want to throttle you, that's a sign you're dealing with a Roller Coaster who is gripped in the anger phase of a radical mood swing. Violent or sustained anger on the part of one or both partners will always reduce the Compatibility Quotient.

How much anger is too much?

Here's a useful rule of thumb: If your potential partner seems to be angry or even irritable more than 5 percent of his or her waking life, you're in for trouble. If you are angry 5 percent of the time, you're probably not ready for marriage, either—at least not to the person who makes you so furious. Also, if bouts of rage come with little or no provocation, the Compatibility Quotient will be commensurately lower.

3. DOES HE OR SHE SEEM EMPTY OR BORED?

In evaluating your answer to this question, you're dealing, once again, with a matter of degree. Everyone gets bored or feels empty or alone from time to time. But the Emotional Roller Coaster seems to feel empty or bored much or all of the time. Most likely, his or her emotional volatility is really a means of compensating for those dead feelings inside.

4. ARE YOU A HERO TO YOUR PARTNER ONE MINUTE, A BUM THE NEXT?

The Roller Coaster sometimes displays a symptom that professional therapists call "splitting." This phenomenon involves a perception that the other partner in the relationship is either all good or all bad. The perception can shift back and forth, from positive to negative, in the blink of an eye.

Here's how it works:

When Charlie met Edie, she seemed totally turned on to him. Everything went wonderfully in the relationship for more than a month, and the couple began to talk seriously of marriage. Edie seemed extremely happy during this period, and Charlie sensed she was deeply in love with him.

But then Charlie forgot one day to return one of Edie's phone calls. To his consternation, she flew into an uncontrollable, accusing rage: "How could you neglect me that way? I was waiting around all evening for your phone call! That was so inconsiderate!"

Of course, the forgotten phone call was only an incidental trigger, an excuse for Edie to fly off the handle. Charlie might have ignored her birthday, or they might have had a mild disagreement over dinner. For almost any reason, Edie was ready to explode, to embark on a precarious upswing and then a careening plunge in her emotions.

Her hero, Charlie, had turned overnight into an unfeeling monster. In the wake of this burst of anger, she actually found herself hating him because she perceived he had neglected her. While she had idealized him in the first weeks of their relationship, she now thought of every reason to despise him. She tore him down unmercifully when they were together, and also when talking with her friends.

Splitting is perhaps the most malignant symptom of the extreme Roller Coaster personality. Those in the grip of this problem have lost control of their thinking processes. As a result, their chances for marital compatibility are poor.

Fortunately for Charlie, he realized that he would be taking too big a chance trying to build a relationship with Edie. He continued to see her for a few weeks after she calmed down, but on at least two other occasions, he noticed signs of similar volatility. So, he broke up with her and began looking for someone with less mercurial emotions.

5. DOES YOUR PARTNER SEEM TO KNOW WHO HE OR SHE REALLY IS?

Those on the emotional roller coaster usually are wrestling with a profound uncertainty about their identity. This problem personality may continually ask, "Who am I? What do I believe in? What kind of friends should I have? What should I do for a living?"

Up to a point, these are normal questions, particularly among young people who are still trying to make some fundamental decisions about the meaning of life. Everyone should give a great deal of thought to the direction in which his or her life is heading.

But there should also be some resolution of basic identity issues as one matures. We believe that a thirty-year-old adult is in trouble, for example, if he still has no idea what his fundamental values are. It's quite possible that some basic questions may remain unanswered beyond this age, but at this point one should have more answers than questions.

For example, you might still wonder about one or two major issues, such as

- Is there a God?
- What's the right, responsible way for me to approach my sexuality?
- What standards of honesty should I follow?
- What career should I pursue?

If you're still casting about with most of these issues, or if you've abandoned any attempt to find answers, then you're at risk for marital problems. A potentially reliable spouse must have a solid sense of his or her value system and code of behavior.

6. DOES YOUR PARTNER HAVE A HISTORY OF WILD MOOD SWINGS?

If you suspect that you're dealing with an Emotional Roller Coaster, it's always helpful to chart your partner's past mood swings. Then, you'll be able to see more clearly whether or not this person has a pattern of problem activity, or just occasionally gets too angry or wild.

Also, as you list the various incidents that you know about or have heard about, note the most serious expressions of despair. Is there a record of suicidal threats or gestures? How about self-mutilating behavior? Does your partner frequently overreact to little problems?

With this overview of your partner's emotional reactions in front of you in black and white, you'll be able to anticipate more clearly what you can expect from week to week and month to month if you decide to enter into a longer-lasting relationship.

In practical terms, what should you do if you're currently involved with an Emotional Roller Coaster?

If you're not yet married, we'd suggest that you proceed with great caution. Try not to fool yourself, such as by rationalizing, "With all her faults, this is still a really exciting person!" It's best not to be too patient or avoid confrontations when your partner slips into a bad mood. Instead, use each negative mood swing as a test case. Respond firmly when your boyfriend or girlfriend acts outrageously.

If you find that your partner can pull back and discuss the problem rationally, the two of you may be compatible after all. If not—if every minor dispute turns into a major crisis—the chances are that there's nothing you can do to change your companion. In such a case, we think you should consider getting out while you're still ahead. Marriage to an Emotional Roller Coaster rarely works out well.

But what if you're already married to such a person?

In that case, the situation becomes more difficult and the possible solutions less clear. In many cases the best initial approach is for the calmer married partner to confront the Roller Coaster with his or her crazy behavior and to try to talk through a mutually agreeable resolution.

If that's not possible, and often it won't be, the next step should be for the couple to seek marriage counseling. As with Meg and Jack, such therapy may involve a long and arduous working through of various problems in the relationship. But sometimes, couples who have the motivation and courage to take this route will experience improvement in their marriage.

The Con Artist

One of the most colorful, yet destructive, high-risk personalities we've encountered is what we call the "Con Artist." Like other problem partners, Con Artists exist on a broad spectrum, from the negligently deceitful to the deeply disturbed sociopath or psychopath.

More often than not, the Con Artist is a man, though certainly some women also qualify. There is a variety of distinctive character and behavior traits that you may find in this type of high-risk partner. Among other things, it's possible that this person

- May be bright, charming, sophisticated and socially adept
- Possesses a strong self-centered, selfish streak and usually has to have his or her own way
- Is quite persuasive with members of the opposite sex

- Lies or fibs easily, with such dazzling rationalizations and justifications that even when you know something is a lie, you want to believe it's true
- At the deepest level, is insensitive to the needs and feelings of others
- Has difficulty empathizing with others
- May seem incapable of admitting he's wrong—*or*, in some instances, may frequently say he's sorry and ask for forgiveness, only to turn around and engage in the same conduct again
- Regards love relationships primarily as a challenge to *get* something from the partner, whether it be sex, money or some other objective

In the most serious cases, the Con Artist may have been in trouble with the law; failed to pay taxes; be a heavy drinker or drug abuser; or have left a string of misled, disappointed lovers or wives in his wake. Sometimes, this person may even be unaware that there's a problem with his behavior. In any case, his tendency is to blame other people or circumstances for his problems or failed relationships.

Here are some comments from a few of the more extreme kinds of Con Artists that we've encountered:

- A dashing young stockbroker mainly dated with the goal of talking as many women as he could into bed: "I'm not ready to get married yet, and I know these girls have fun while they're with me. Sure, most of them probably want to get married, and I guess I do lead them on during the early part of the relationship. But that's what dating is all about, isn't it? You know, all's fair in love and war, and all that. Besides, I just may get serious with one of these girls someday!"
- A man with a long history of cheating on his wife told us that he never really meant to do it: "These women I got involved with were all so seductive. I'm just weak, and I can't resist."

- Another tried to explain to his wife why they were being audited for the fourth time in four years by the Internal Revenue Service: "I don't know why they're picking on me. Everyone cheats on taxes."
- A young woman who had collected jewelry (including engagement rings) and other gifts from a string of boyfriends she had dumped expressed her philosophy this way: "Dating carries with it certain expectations. A girl is supposed to get presents, and if a guy isn't willing to give them, he shouldn't even try to get involved in serious relationships."
- A young man talked his girlfriend into charging hundreds of dollars for him on her credit card, then jilted her with this comment: "I told her that I was nervous about using someone else's credit card, but she insisted that it was okay with her. I said I might have trouble paying the money back, but she said, 'Oh, don't worry about it. I'm not a collection agency.' So who can blame me?"

Con Artists are impulsive, egocentric, irresponsible and immature. They often seem to lack a conscience, or at least have rationalized away the capacity to feel normal guilt, remorse or shame. Yet when they are wooing their romantic prey, they can seem so sincere and sensitive that it may become very difficult to break away from them.

If you unwittingly get involved with one of these people, you can expect your Compatibility Quotient to plummet.

Rosemarie's Encounter with the Con Artist

Rosemarie, a twenty-three-year-old who had just graduated from college, came from an immigrant family. Her father had died when she was only six, a circumstance which had resulted in a strong relationship with her mother, but an uncertain, unconfident attitude when she was around men. She was a pleasant-looking woman, with a trim, some might even say sexy, figure. But she seemed unusually intense in conversations and reacted in a jumpy, disconcerted way to new people and situations.

Rosemarie's mother was a clever and inventive person who had opened a small grocery store which eventually turned out to be a small gold mine. Being an astute businesswoman, she had managed to turn a significant profit year after year, as well as provide herself with a substantial salary. Now, her modest home was paid off and she had a sizable nest egg for her own retirement and an estate to pass on to Rosemarie and her older sister.

Rosemarie had begun working at the store while she was in high school and had continued to shoulder increasing responsibilities there while she attended a nearby college. Then, after graduation, she took over many of the management duties from her mother.

Neither the education she received nor the money she was making in the family business, however, did much for her self-image. She still felt awkward and unattractive and secretly referred to herself as a "little mouse."

Objectively speaking, Rosemarie was being quite hard on herself. In fact, she didn't lack for dates or offers of dates, but these came from young men she had known all her life in her neighborhood.

"I can't seem to break out of this environment," she said more than once. "I don't want a local boy for a husband."

In other words, she knew she could attract men from her own social stratum, but she had aspirations for someone with better education and more occupational potential. She devalued the local men as much as she devalued herself.

What Rosemarie *thought* she wanted was a young man who had graduated from one of the best schools and had the potential to go to the top in his field. She wanted someone who was suave, sophisticated and maybe even a little exotic—but above all, a man who had the capacity to take her with him to the aeries of financial success and social status.

Then, Sam entered her life. Sam was a handsome young fellow who began to shop regularly at the grocery store and happened to meet Rosemarie when he asked about getting a line of credit there. Rosemarie, who had to approve his application, was immediately smitten.

Sam dressed exactly as she had always imagined an upwardly

mobile man should dress. His immaculate suits and beautiful silk ties were always perfectly matched. No hair was ever out of place. He moved gracefully, and he always appeared to be "up."

In their initial conversation, Sam had casually identified himself as "a financial consultant" and made it a point to indicate that he had attended one of the nation's leading business schools. "But I didn't go back for my final year because I received one of those 'offers you can't refuse,' if you know what I mean."

Rosemarie *didn't* know exactly, but the explanation sounded impressive enough to her. In any event, she approved the application without further delay.

When Sam asked her for a date a few days after they met, Rosemarie felt like a twittery teenager. She could hardly wait for the big day to arrive, and when Sam finally pulled up in front of her home in his expensive foreign car, she had a definite sense that "this is the one for me!"

Sam had a way of choosing eating spots and entertainment that somehow fulfilled all Rosemarie's fantasies. They went to an exotic French restaurant that first night—"Reminds me of the many weeks I've spent in Paris," he confided. Then, they attended an outdoor concert—"Music like this somehow gets down deep inside me, helps me think more seriously about the things in life that really matter."

Rosemarie was enthralled by what she interpreted as Sam's broad interests, obvious intelligence and sensitivity. She decided almost immediately that this was a guy that she didn't want to allow to get away. It was easy for her to agree to accompany him to his apartment and engage in sex on that first date. Then, they shared a nightcap and enjoyed a little more dreamy music on his state-of-the-art stereo before she left for home.

The couple continued to date fairly regularly, at least once a week, and after about a month, he started to talk about marriage. Rosemarie could hardly believe her good fortune. "Why would this handsome, sharp guy be so interested in me?" she puzzled. "But I'm not about to question it. Of course I'll marry him if he wants me."

But Sam didn't want to enter into a formal engagement just yet, he said. "We've got time, and I want to be sure everything is just right with my career before we begin to set dates. In the meantime, it's almost the same as being married, don't you think?"

In fact, Rosemarie *didn't* think their relationship was like a marriage. They saw each other only once a week, and it seemed that she was paying for more and more of their activities. She was sure she loved Sam, though, and above all, she didn't want to rock the boat.

Her mother, however, wasn't nearly as enchanted, to put it mildly. She actually had been quite suspicious of Sam from the first day she met him. She couldn't clearly articulate the reasons for her concern, except to say, "He's not like us. He doesn't seem to fit into our family very well."

In what Rosemarie regarded as a classic case of majoring in minors, Mom found herself focusing on the young man's perfectly manicured fingernails. "Where I come from, no working man paints his nails with that clear polish," she explained. "Sure, I know he's supposed to have this big job, but somehow, those nails just seem *too* nice."

Rosemarie had always followed her mother's advice in the past, but this time, she turned a deaf ear to the warnings. Even when Sam began to ask her for cash loans, she disregarded all the teachings her mother had given her about "not dipping into your capital."

Instead, she withdrew hundreds of dollars from her savings, believing without question when Sam told her that business reverses had put him "temporarily in an embarrassing situation." He assured her, "With my education and experience, I'll be back on my feet in no time. And when things get better, I'll pay this money back with premium interest!" Rosemarie protested that the interest wouldn't be necessary and as a matter of fact, she added, "What's a loan between two people who are going to be married?"

After their relationship had been going on for nearly a year, Rosemarie found that she had become virtually a slave to the financial and sexual demands of her boyfriend. Practically every time they got together, she brought him some article of clothing, a sack of groceries or a cash loan. Also, when he suggested that she might want to invest some money in a project he was working on, she immediately wrote him a check for the amount he suggested.

As for their social life, it had become virtually nonexistent. Sam only seemed interested in getting her into bed and then sending her home by herself after their weekly get-together. And he constantly resisted meeting her any more often—"I have too many business demands on me at the moment. I'm often traveling and have to work late hours."

Throughout their acquaintanceship, Sam had been reticent to discuss his background, his other friends or his work. Whenever Rosemarie probed a little to find out more about him, he dodged her questions with a comment like, "Oh, that's boring. Let's talk about something more interesting. Let's talk about us."

Finally, when Sam had obtained nearly $20,000 from Rosemarie in loans and "investments"—and this didn't include the food and other handouts she had given him—he seemed to become more testy than ever when she suggested firming up their engagement. At that point, something snapped inside her.

"Something's really wrong here," she decided. She decided to do some checking.

She tried to find out something about the small consulting company where Sam said he worked, but she found no such business listed in the phone book. Then, she made a special, unannounced trip over to Sam's apartment on one of their "off" days when he said he would be working. To her shock, when she rang the intercom in his apartment, a woman's voice answered.

Rosemarie was so devastated she didn't know what to do at first. She just stood outside Sam's apartment in a daze for several minutes. Finally, still trembling, she went to her car, drove home and brooded about what course of action to take.

Rosemarie was reluctant to disclose to her mother just how much money Sam had borrowed or how far their sexual relationship had developed, so she sought help from a psychotherapist. His advice in a nutshell: You're in over your head. Confront this guy, and find out exactly who he is and what his intentions are; then try to get your money back. And whatever happens, get out of the relationship.

At their next scheduled rendezvous at his apartment, Rosemarie did ask Sam some very direct questions about his work and his other relationships, including his connection with the woman whose voice she had heard on the intercom. His response: "How can you question me this way? I'm a consultant; I'm always in touch with clients. As a matter of fact, I've been working on building my own company. That firm I used to be with has dissolved. But your investments are doing quite well. You just have to trust me."

"What about the woman? Who was she?"

"Look, Rosie, I told you, I have a lot of clients, and I have to meet them here in the apartment since I don't have a regular office. I must have been on the phone working on another deal when you rang. This place is a madhouse during the week. That's why we can meet only once a week."

Rosemarie backed off. Sam was so strong and persuasive, and she so wanted him to be what her fantasies had told her he was.

Unfortunately, Sam turned out to be what almost any objective observer would recognize him for—a consummate Con Artist. After several additional months of anxiety, tears and unhappiness, Rosemarie was able to piece a more complete picture together:

Sam *had* attended a leading business school, but had hopped around among several jobs and in effect was unemployed during the period when Rosemarie knew him. To be sure, he had high aspirations and expectations for himself, but he lacked the commitment and stability necessary to bring his dreams to reality. Instead, he continued a habit he had fallen into years before— preying on young women, including Rosemarie.

The three women friends he was currently involved with had lent him nearly $50,000 in the course of a little over a year, and of course, they never saw the money again. Each went to Sam's apartment on a different night, and for months they never crossed paths. Rosemarie was the one who exploded the complex arrangement.

She had finally concluded that Sam was going too far in his financial demands when he asked her to convince her mother to invest money in a limited partnership. "This particular deal requires a minimum investment of $40,000, but maybe I can get you two into it with a little less."

She refused on the spot, and furthermore, found she was strangely unmoved when he seemed miffed. For the first time she found she was able to say to herself, "If he's rejecting me because I've turned down this deal, so be it!"

As far as their physical fidelity to each other was concerned, her suspicions had already been aroused by that female "client" she talked to on the intercom. Then, one evening she accidentally saw Sam's distinctive sports car when she was out shopping in his neighborhood. This time, he was with a "client" who was blond, young and buxom. Rosemarie followed them to his apartment, where Sam ushered the woman out of the car and into the building, all the while holding hands and caressing her.

When Rosemarie got together with Sam the next night, she confronted him with what she had seen, but this time, he merely shrugged his shoulders. "Look, Rosie, I have a strong sex drive. There are some things you won't do with me, and I have my needs. Now, if you think we might get a little more creative in bed . . ."

But Sam didn't get any further. Rosemarie was already on her way out the door. She finally understood the situation. With the help of her therapist and her mother, she put this relationship behind her and began to experience some healing of the emotional wounds she had suffered.

"How could I have been so naive?" she berated herself in the days and weeks immediately following the breakup. "How could I ever have believed him? The guy is obviously sick, but how could I have allowed myself to be fooled this way?"

The answer to this question is that in matters of love and marriage, *many* people are fooled by Con Artists. The deceptions almost always succeed because the victim *wants* to believe what she hears. She has an image in her mind about the ideal mate, and it's easy to overlook faults, flaws, and CQ danger signals—even the really big and obvious ones—when some of the ingredients in the perfect marriage seem present.

As for the Con Artist, he is often an intentional deceiver. But many times, he also deceives himself. Certainly, he's always selfish and out to satisfy his own needs, whether they are sexual, financial or in some other realm. At the same time, though, he may convince himself that he's not so bad. Here are the kinds of mind games he plays with himself:

- "This girl is getting something out of the relationship too"; or
- "Those are the risks of a romantic relationship"; or
- "I'm not sure what I want in a love relationship, and there's no better way to find out than to experiment."

Yet whatever the Con Artist's rationalizations, motives or even redeeming characteristics, it's his victim who suffers most. The women (and occasionally men) who get into trouble with this type of problem partner are easily manipulated because the Con Artist has an uncanny ability to make others feel special. They are seductive and know how to please. When crossed, however, they'll "shut down" emotionally, blame the other partner and sometimes even turn violent.

How Can You Identify the Con Artist?

As you may have noticed, a number of the questions we included in the Compatibility Quotient questionnaire relate to the dangers posed by the Con Artist. For example, we wanted you to determine the extent to which you and your partner are trusting, responsible, honest and open about personal backgrounds. If you or your companion scored low on these and similar items, there may be a Con Artist in your midst!

Ironically, the more honest, trusting and open you are, the more likely you are to be fooled. One way to begin to establish an identification of the Con Artist is to watch just how flattering he is to you. How aggressively does he try to ingratiate himself or win you over? Check to see if his conversation is filled at an *early* point in your relationship with statements like these:

- "You're the greatest woman in the world."
- "You and only you can make me happy."
- "Your kind of love could easily make an honest man out of me."
- "There are no limits to what the two of us could do to-gether."

Then, begin to watch how this man's demands on you escalate. Even as you're being flattered and built up verbally, does he seem to be pressing you excessively to have sex with him? Do you sense that one of his primary interests is to have you satisfy certain physical appetites or other needs? In short, do you have a lurking sense that you're being used by this person?

The presence of these two factors—excessive flattery combined with a feeling that you're being used—should cause danger signals to go off in your mind. In these circumstances, the chances are very good that you're dealing with a Con Artist.

If you're still unsure and want to probe further, see how your partner stacks up with the following six-point checklist. And remember: Although female Con Artists are less common, they do exist. So whenever we use the masculine pronoun in the following text, men may want to plug in the feminine, just to see how their companion checks out.

1. DOES HE TELL THE TRUTH?

Almost everyone lies or bends the truth, at least once in a while. Beware, though, if your partner has no regard for the truth. For example, you might ask these questions:

- Does he tell truth and falsehood with equal facility, depending on which approach suits his purposes at a given time? Constant and adept "storytelling" may signal a chronic problem with deception.
- How much remorse does he show when caught? The fact that your partner is capable of feeling ashamed when you

confront him with an impropriety may be a good sign. Also, a normal person may be tempted to cover up some shameful act with a fib because he knows he's behaved wrongly and doesn't want others to think poorly of him. The genuine Con Artist, however, is never really embarrassed, even if he's caught red-handed.

- Does he occasionally tell small untruths, or is he deceptive about the things that really count? Occasional fibs or white lies are quite normal, particularly if they're intended to explain away embarrassing or unpleasant behavior. It may not be too bad for a person to fib that he's had to work late, and that's why he forgot the groceries. But if he tells you that he had to work late when in fact he was fired two weeks ago—that's quite different!

2. DOES HE TEND TO BE RESPONSIBLE, PARTICULARLY ABOUT MONEY?

Money is often the Con Artist's weak spot. For some, everything is measured in terms of money. They may assume there's really no such thing as loyalty or friendship without a price.

Again, making a judgment in this area is a matter of degree. Occasional irresponsibility, particularly if the stakes are not too high, may be cause for only mild annoyance. On the other hand, you must be much more cautious with the person who never does what he is supposed to do, and in general cannot be relied upon.

Also, beware of unpaid bills. A common excuse by the Con Artist: "Those damned credit card companies just can't keep their files straight!" Most people find themselves hating credit card companies at one time or another, and many have suffered from computer foul-ups. So this kind of complaint has a great deal of plausibility. Be cautious, however, if you hear these excuses too often.

If you're really worried about whether your partner is financially responsible, you may have to check around a bit. For example, an attorney should be able to run a discreet check on your partner's credit status.

3. IS HE RECKLESS ABOUT HIS PERSONAL BEHAVIOR?

Ask yourself if your partner is a compulsive thrill seeker. (In fact, you've already responded to this question in the CQ questionnaire.) For example, does he consistently drive too fast, or drive while drinking, seemingly unconcerned about the consequences? There's nothing wrong with an exciting personality. The issue here, though, is whether or not this person can behave responsibly and accept the fact that there are consequences to his acts.

4. HAS HE EVER SUSTAINED A MONOGAMOUS RELATIONSHIP FOR AT LEAST SIX MONTHS?

Your partner may tell you that you're the one and only person he has ever cared for, and that may be true and quite commendable.

We would become concerned, however, if he's been involved with many women, but has never established a relationship that has lasted more than two months—particularly if he's over twenty-five. A past history of brief or unstable intimate relationships—perhaps including bouts of promiscuity—will be a pretty reliable indicator that his Compatibility Quotient is dangerously low.

5. WHAT IS YOUR PARTNER'S WORK HISTORY?

Again, you've responded to this issue in the CQ questionnaire. But now is a good time to return to the topic and explore it in greater depth.

Ask yourself: Has he ever held a job for a reasonable length of time, or has he moved from one position to another rather rapidly? There are many good reasons for switching jobs, but there are also many bad ones.

Also, be cautious if, in his explanations for moving about, he indicates that he was always in the right and bosses and coworkers were always in the wrong. For example, a warning light should go on in your head if he tells you that every boss he ever worked for was a no-good jerk, and he was always justified in walking out.

6. HAS HE EVER BEEN IN TROUBLE WITH THE LAW?

In our practice we've seen women fascinated by men who have been in trouble with the law. Some even go so far as to marry them. But these marriages are usually brief and extremely unhappy.

Anyone can make a mistake, of course, and there are plenty of people who learn a good lesson after they've been caught doing illegal acts. For that matter, ex-convicts may reform their ways completely. But such cases are few and far between. Most of the time, the Con Artist simply doesn't learn from experience.

Typical protests by the deceivers who have been caught:

"It was all a frame-up."
Or, "I was hanging out with bad people."
Or, "I was in the wrong place at the wrong time."
Or, "The jury made a terrible mistake."
Or, "The government is just hounding me."

The Con Artist will offer these and other hollow excuses which he knows are false, but which he thinks he can seduce you into believing. But don't be fooled! In general, those who cross the line into actual criminal behavior are extremely bad risks for marriage.

Finally, if you decide you're dealing with a Con Artist, don't think that you can change him. The odds are overwhelmingly against you.

Unfortunately, too many of those who are overeager to get married shut their eyes to the obvious and take the plunge. They ignore the advice of parents and friends, as well as their own good judgment. In an orgy of wishful thinking, they succumb to the seduction, and the experience often feels good for a while. But believe us, that feeling won't last!

In the last analysis, you have to be tough in dealing with a person you suspect is a Con Artist. Ask the hard, uncomfortable questions. Demand concrete evidence, and check it out. The wise person will always measure a potential partner against realities, facts and sound moral standards, even as she revels in the wonders of romance.

SIX

The Suspicious Suitor

The muggings, burglaries and assorted other crimes plaguing our cities and suburbs should alert us that we live in a dangerous society. For that reason, it's important for every wise citizen to become "street smart," or able to sense and respond to the threats that lurk about. Without good antennae, we become more vulnerable to assault or abuse.

Most normal human beings are biologically and culturally equipped to distinguish friend from foe. Of course, some people are a little more trusting than others, and some are a little more suspicious. For the most part, though, we can separate the world into those people and situations that are dangerous, and those that are not. In other words, we can strike a balance between those who basically love and support us, and those who are real threats—between trust and wariness.

But the suspicious nature of some people may become dominant to one degree or another and produce the problem personality that we've labeled the Suspicious Suitor. In more clinical terms, this person is paranoid. That is, he loses his bearings about which people or situations are worthy of his trust, and which are not.

The paranoid disorders are in some ways the most human of mental aberrations. Animals innately seem to know who or what to trust. Only humans turn against their best friends and accuse them of plotting and perfidy, perhaps on the thinnest of evidence.

There is a wide range of paranoid disorders, some of which are part of quite serious and pervasive mental conditions. Paranoid schizophrenia, for example, is marked by bizarre behavior, delusional beliefs, and an inability to separate what is real from what is not. On the other hand, there are less serious forms of paranoia characterized by unwarranted suspicion and mistrust. Those are the ones we're mainly concerned with here.

The Suspicious Suitor—a paranoid type who can completely undercut the Compatibility Quotient in a love relationship—is always on the watch for wrongs, slights or threats. Usually a male, but not always, he or she has a number of typical traits:

- He seems to *expect* that he will be tricked or harmed.
- She has a special facility for reading hostility, criticism or hidden motives into the most innocent actions or words of others.
- He tends to be more jealous than most people.
- She's more pessimistic than optimistic.
- She prides herself on being highly rational and may seem cold or emotionless, uncomfortable with expressions of sentiment or tenderness.
- He lacks a sense of humor.
- He's quick to take offense and to counterattack when he thinks he's under threat.
- During initial encounters, he may seem unusually interested in you, or intensely warm, caring and flattering—with the suspicious side of his nature emerging more clearly after you get to know each other better.

How Vicki Was Trapped by a Suspicious Suitor

Vicki clearly remembers her first date with Mark. She met him in a singles bar, and they soon were deeply involved in a fascinating conversation about their mutual interest in literature and art. She was particularly impressed by the broad range of cultural experiences and travel he enjoyed on his job. To top it all off, Mark was a great dancer, and dancing was one of Vicki's favorite pastimes. With all these common interests, Vicki soon began to think she might have found the right man for marriage.

Their first few evenings together had a special glow, as Vicki basked in Mark's overt displays of affection and his obvious intelligence and sophistication. As a result, she became more and more convinced that she had found the person with whom she wanted to spend the rest of her life.

Certain little things went almost unnoticed during those early dates, though Vicki remembered them later when she was describing their relationship during therapy. For example, Mark pointedly ignored her friends at one party, despite the fact that they had all been sitting together most of the evening. On that occasion, he had insisted on leaving the party early with Vicki, and she had reluctantly agreed, though she could easily have spent another hour at the get-together. Also, at a small dinner party a week or so later, Mark had been rude to one of his own friends who complimented Vicki on her dress. That time they left early again, also at Mark's urging.

At first, Vicki couldn't quite figure out these reactions because she had always been gregarious and extremely independent. Her father had adored her and given her everything she wanted; while she was a senior in high school, her family had even sent her abroad to study. For the last seven years since graduating from college, she had lived in her own apartment and done pretty much as she had pleased with the money from her well-paying job.

Vicki had often been the center of attention in her large family and among her many close friends. Also, she was accustomed to being admired by her boyfriends, and in general, Mark's ardor seemed just a continuation of the high esteem she had always enjoyed.

On the other hand, she found herself becoming somewhat disconcerted by some of his more extreme and effusive compliments, such as, "You're the most gorgeous woman who ever lived." Vicki knew she was reasonably attractive, but the "most gorgeous ever"? That seemed a little much.

Still, she found it was rather nice to be put on such a pedestal. So, despite some of the questions she still had about him, she enthusiastically accepted when Mark proposed marriage.

Things started to go wrong almost from the moment of their engagement. The first bad argument Vicki remembered occurred over the wedding preparations. Mark became obsessed with who was sitting next to whom, and what situations or topics might be the subject of gossip. For the most part, Vicki shrugged off these concerns, though she gave in to Mark when he seemed exceptionally worried about a particular person or table arrangement.

As time wore on, Mark also seemed to pick more fights with Vicki's friends. He was especially resentful of Walter, a man she had dated briefly in high school. Walter was now married and had three kids, and over the years he and Vicki had developed a warm, nonsexual friendship.

"For the last time, there has been nothing between Walter and me for ten years!" Vicki told Mark in exasperation. "Besides, if I were carrying on an affair with him, would I do it under your nose? I've known him all my life!"

"I know," Mark replied, giving in to some extent on this point. "But it still makes me uneasy."

Mark continued to shower Vicki with declarations of his love. But after they had been married several months, she began to feel strangely uncomfortable with these words of affection.

"How can I feel so unloved when he's always telling me he adores me?" she wondered.

Mark then objected when she had to work late several nights in a row. Among other things, he made snide remarks about the attractive guys in her office. He also protested when she decided to go on a weekend church retreat without him.

"What are the living accommodations up there?" he asked. "How about the social activities? Do they have swimming or hiking planned in the woods? Just be sure to always have a couple of other women around you."

Things really fell apart when their baby was born. Mark's jealousy was now boundless, yet he had no plausible excuse. His complaint? He was bitterly resentful that Vicki was spending more time with the infant than with him. It soon became clear that he was fearful of being displaced by his own son.

Mark was displaying some classic signs of the paranoid personality. Certainly, his suspicious nature wasn't serious enough to warrant institutionalization, but it was sufficiently aggravating to inflict steady, pounding damage on his marriage and other relationships.

With Vicki, his paranoia had emerged in the form of extreme possessiveness and jealousy. At work, the manifestations were a little different. He frequently sensed that coworkers or bosses were "out to get me." In fact, his suspicions often alienated his colleagues to the point that they became self-fulfilling prophecies: The more he assumed he was being threatened or rejected, the more he actually was threatened and rejected. He lost at least one promotion opportunity because of his excessively suspicious and untrusting nature.

The marriage was in even more trouble. Vicki, finding that her need for independence and "space" was being destroyed by her husband's distrust, finally decided that she had had enough. She left Mark just before their baby's first birthday, and for several weeks, she even refused to take his calls. They finally decided to try some marriage counseling, but things had gone too far. Legal action ensued, and the two are now divorced.

Why did Mark behave as he did? Here's a more in-depth look at what was going on inside him:

- As you can readily surmise from the above descriptions of their relationship, Mark was terrified that Vicki was going to dump him.

- However, he couldn't stand being so dependent. From his frame of reference, this sort of fear was "unmanly."
- A major reason for Mark's worries about abandonment was that he had deep-seated doubts about his own attractiveness. Therefore, he always assumed that his partner would be attracted to someone (*anyone*) else.
- For these reasons, Mark was always jealous and suspected that every innocent encounter must mean that Vicki would leave.

Suspicious Suitors like Mark can sometimes keep a marriage together if they're involved with someone less independent than Vicki. In many cases, however, their partners become exasperated by their possessiveness and lack of trust, and the relationship breaks up. It's a sad irony that the paranoid character often continues to love his partner, even when the marriage is in deep trouble. In effect, he ends up alienating the very person he cares for the most.

How Suspicious Suitors Undercut the Compatibility Quotient

Members of either sex may fall into the Suspicious Suitor category and may be identified through a number of questions we included on the Compatibility Quotient. For example, several of the items dealt with trust, suspicion, jealousy and responses to criticism. Related questions include those on the reaction to being alone, working closely with members of the opposite sex and traveling away from home for extended periods of time.

In general, there are four main themes that underlie most of these paranoia-related questions on the Compatibility Quotient. These include (1) serious jealousy, (2) the subordination of trust to suspicion, (3) projection onto a loved one of one's own weaknesses, and (4) the power of pessimism over optimism.

THEME 1: SERIOUS JEALOUSY.

Serious or unreasonable jealousy, a common trait of the Suspicious Suitor, puts unbearable pressure on a marriage. It's the paranoid man who is usually jealous, and his wife can never seem to shake the cloud of suspicion and doubt that he generates.

"Where were you yesterday?" he asks slyly. "Why is the odometer showing a hundred miles more than usual? Who is the man who called last week? Do you really have to go out alone?"

No amount of reassurance, no amount of evidence will prevent the really serious paranoid character from embarking on his next episode of doubt and blame.

Serious jealousy of this type has sometimes been called the "Othello Syndrome," after Shakespeare's unhappy Moor, who strangled his beloved wife because she couldn't prove she was innocent of betrayal. Even as he killed her, he knew he loved her, but he couldn't stop himself. Only with her dying breath did he see the magnitude of his mistake—and then, he killed himself.

Of course, murder isn't the problem the typical companion of the Suspicious Suitor should worry about. Most paranoid characters aren't violent at all. They simply make themselves and their partners miserable by their constant mistrust. The reason: They cannot compensate for their deep-seated sense of low self-worth. Therefore, they always suspect that others are trying to do them in.

THEME 2: SUSPICION OVER TRUST.

A dimension of human behavior that appears to be associated with remaining married is the ability to trust another person. Trust includes the ability to have positive opinions about the helpfulness, fairness and reliability of other people. As a matter of fact, there's a direct correlation between the capacity for trust and marital satisfaction.

In her book *Married People: Staying Together in the Age of Divorce*, Francine Klagsbrun studied eighty-seven couples who had made it happily for fifteen years or more. Klagsbrun tried to distill the basic ingredients of a happy marriage and answer the eternal question, "What is the key to success in a relationship?"

She found no perfect formula. But she was able to identify a few basic common factors among the pairs in her sample.

Top among the qualities that bound a couple together was trust. "Feelings of love may wax and wane," wrote Klagsbrun, but "trust is a constant; without it there is no true marriage. Trust forms the basis for security and comfort. Trust also makes it possible, in the words of psychiatrist Aaron Stein, for both partners 'to be themselves and have their own feelings.' And in this safety lies a special kind of freedom."

Trust is no mere abstraction or impractical value that won't work in the real world. Rather, trust is an essential tool. It permits two people to straddle the sticky pockets of an imperfect, shared existence and avoid getting mired in all the little doubts and problems that are bound to occur. Normal people with the capacity to trust don't worry if a spouse comes home late from work, plans an out-of-town business trip or attends meetings at church or charity committees where members of the opposite sex are present.

Hardened Suspicious Suitors, on the other hand, cannot trust. It's not that they don't want to trust; their problem is that they really *can't* trust. For example, a wife may prove herself innocent for the hundredth time. That may make the paranoid husband feel ashamed, and he'll vow to trust her on the next occasion. But eventually, he'll lapse back into his old suspicions because fears of abandonment overwhelm him.

Any small, innocent event may trigger his mistrust. He may answer the phone and find that the person on the other end hangs up at the sound of his voice. Or he may come across a letter in the mail addressed to his wife, but with a strange return address. Or she may appear one day in a new outfit or a different perfume. It takes little for the Suspicious Suitor to emerge once again.

THEME 3: PROJECTION.

It was Freud who first noted that the roots of paranoia lie deep in the mind of the suspicious person himself. This individual may be scared or worried about something, but he can't face the things he fears. Instead, he projects them onto someone else.

For example, a married man may become attracted to another

woman. He can't acknowledge his lust openly, and he may not even be able to acknowledge it to himself. But he can't completely ignore it or get rid of it with a snap of the fingers. So suddenly, without a bit of concrete proof, he finds himself suspecting his wife of flirting. Perhaps he even accuses her of infidelity. The Suspicious Suitor assumes this attitude not out of a conscious effort to manipulate his partner. In fact, he really *believes* there's some basis for his suspicions.

A less dramatic illustration is the woman who has unsuccessfully struggled with feelings of inadequacy and ends up projecting them onto her spouse. She begins to see her husband as incapable and unambitious. Yet this woman is really expressing the feelings and doubts she has about herself and her own passivity.

The process of projection turns internal conflict into marital blame. People end up finding fault with uncomprehending partners for the horrors that lurk in their own souls.

In the short term, if you determine that your partner's main problem is such projection, you may decide, "Well, that's not so bad. He's a reasonable person, and if I just explain what's happening, it's likely that he'll change and our relationship will get back on track." If you're not yet married and you're deeply involved romantically, you may fool yourself into believing that your loved one *will* change, perhaps with your help.

In the long run, however, projection is usually just a first step toward big problems. It's very difficult to overcome a deeply ingrained paranoia, other than through intensive therapy. In most cases, when this particular theme of the Suspicious Suitor is present, the marriage will self-destruct. So if you're not yet married and you find that your partner is given to frequent bouts of projection, it will probably be best for you to get out of the relationship.

THEME 4: THE PREVALENCE OF PESSIMISM.

A number of studies have shown that married people tend to be more optimistic than those who are unattached. They are more optimistic to begin with, and they remain so throughout the marriage.

Research also has revealed that married people are more satisfied with life in general than are single people. Married couples report greater contentment with everything from hobbies to friendships to work. To put this another way, a person's natural optimism and satisfaction with life contribute greatly to the development of a happy marriage. Furthermore, those who are naturally content tend to stay married. They seem to take life as it comes, without too much complaining.

The Suspicious Suitor, on the other hand, is a born pessimist. He assumes that everything will turn out badly. Pessimists project their chronic dissatisfaction onto their marriage; then they desert or drive their partners away. So, pessimism, along with the other three themes we've mentioned, tends to reduce the Compatibility Quotient.

How to Spot the Suspicious Suitor—And Test the Seriousness of His Problem

As we've said, Suspicious Suitors exist on a wide spectrum of behavior, from the mildly wary to the intensely paranoid. Many times, a slightly suspicious person may be coaxed and loved back into a better and more trusting emotional balance. On the other hand, the deeply ingrained paranoid will usually be impervious to any efforts to change his personality.

So, how can you spot the Suspicious Suitor and determine whether or not he may be open to change?

In addition to evaluating the results of your Compatibility Quotient, this six-question checklist should help you make an evaluation.

1. DOES HE BEAR A GRUDGE?

A red flag that signals the presence of a hard-to-change Suspicious Suitor is the habit of unreasonably bearing grudges against other people, or holding things against them for long or indefinite periods of time. Of course, we all get angry and may even hold grudges for limited periods. But if a person continues to hold a grudge, and worse, holds several long-term grudges—often despite the possibility of forgiveness or resolution of the bad feelings—then real paranoia may be involved.

Here are some typical responses that may indicate the presence of a serious Suspicious Suitor:

- The entrenched paranoid never forgets—at least not the bad things. He doesn't like his Aunt Daisy because she forgot his birthday when he was six. She's not on speaking terms with her only sister because the sister forgot a dinner date last year. He complains continuously that he was cheated on a business deal or a car purchase.
- When you have a fight, it takes her a long time to get over it.
- He rarely if ever says "I'm sorry."
- She worries for long periods over feelings of dissatisfaction.
- He often "pulls out his garbage bag" when you have an argument. That is, he brings up past complaints, even though the two of you had apparently resolved them long ago.

If you determine that your partner has some of these problems, yet she's willing to talk about them and try to change, that may bode well for a future relationship. On the other hand, if there's no sign of a willingness to work through bad feelings together, or if your partner constantly reverts to holding grudges against you, it's better to forget marriage and move on to another relationship.

Note: As we've indicated earlier, if you're already married to a person with deep-rooted paranoia, your best hope of saving the relationship is professional counseling, either for your spouse alone or even better, for the two of you.

2. DOES HE DISPLAY AN UNUSUAL AMOUNT OF PREJUDICE?

A more subtle sign of paranoia, which can have negative fallout in a love relationship, is outspoken racial or religious bigotry. Here's how it works:

Cary was obviously filled with angry feelings, though he

couldn't admit them to himself or discuss them with the people who were closest to him. Instead, he projected his rage onto unseen strangers, including those of other ethnic backgrounds.

"The blacks [or on other occasions, the Irish or the Turks] are dangerous, and I'm telling you, we have to watch out for them," he declared on a number of occasions to his girlfriend.

Cary was really talking about his own anger, including his frustrations with his lack of achievement and his feelings of inadequacy in his job. But instead of confronting himself, he directed his hostile, negative feelings toward people he had never met.

In this case, his woman friend did well to get out of the relationship, because Cary wasn't the kind of person who would change easily.

The suspicious person may also project other negative emotions onto unfamiliar groups of people. For example, he'll tell you "they're oversexed," or "they're cheap," or "they're stupid." Translated, this means: "I fear that I am undersexed; I'm ashamed that I am cheap or a poor money manager; I'm concerned that I may not be all that bright."

Where prejudice becomes a way of life and a regular characteristic of everyday conversation, the chances are that this attitude permeates the individual's personality. In such a case, you're dealing with an extremely poor risk for a happy marriage.

To test how severe your partner's prejudices really are, confront him. Tell him that you find his attitudes offensive. Then watch his reaction.

Is he capable of backing down and softening his position? If not, you can bet his anger and suspiciousness won't remain confined to strangers. Sooner or later, he'll lash out at you as well.

3. DOES SHE CONSTANTLY OR DEEPLY QUESTION YOUR LOYALTY OR THE LOYALTY OF LONG-TERM FRIENDS AND FAMILY MEMBERS?

Loyalty is a cornerstone of any strong relationship, romantic or otherwise. Those who are incapable of accepting others as loyal are usually doomed to destroy those personal ties.

Jealousy tends to be the primary emotion that rears its ugly head when loyalty comes under fire in a dating or marriage relationship. Of course, all romantic relationships contain at least a little bit of jealousy, but the deeply paranoid person seems always to be jealous.

To evaluate your partner, ask yourself these questions:

- Does he interpret most routine male-female contacts as potentially illicit liaisons?
- Does she constantly check up on you, or question you incessantly about how you spent your day?
- Does she frequently express doubts about your loyalty or that of other people?
- Has he ever turned against a good friend because of a suspicion that that person is taking advantage of him?
- Has she questioned the motivation of relatives or work associates—perhaps even including family members whom she has known all her life, and with whom she has apparently enjoyed a good relationship? Those who are willing to overturn a long-term relationship on the basis of one misunderstanding are poor risks for marriage.

4. DOES HE OVERREACT TO SLIGHTS?

The very Suspicious Suitor may often offend or alienate others, and also tends to be extremely thin-skinned when it comes to observations about himself. He typically takes every general comment personally, as though the person speaking had some hidden meaning or agenda toward him.

5. DOES SHE HAVE GREAT DIFFICULTY IN BEING GOOD-NATURED ABOUT JOKES PLAYED ON HER?

In general, you don't want to joke with the Suspicious Suitor. She's all too likely to take you seriously. She probably can laugh when fun is poked at others, but she usually reacts extremely poorly if she suspects others are laughing at her.

6. IS HE ABLE TO CONFIDE IN YOU?

After a number of dates, the extremely Suspicious Suitor may declare he is wildly in love and that he wants to marry you and share himself completely in the relationship.

To test his sincerity, try asking him, "By the way, how much money do you earn?"—and watch for the reaction.

Some of the responses to this question that have been reported to us in counseling those involved with a suspicious companion are

- A nervous laugh, and quick change of subject
- "Why do you want to know?"
- "Why do you ask?"
- "Is that important to you?"

Questions about money are not particularly romantic. But if a man claims that he loves you and if you're past your first few dates, you're at a stage in the relationship where sharing intimate matters has become appropriate. Defensiveness about money could be a danger signal.

Chances are you'll get a similar reaction about other emotion-laden subjects. The Suspicious Suitor may be evasive in telling you about his family, his work or other aspects of his background.

Of course, many people who are not particularly suspicious may have trouble talking about certain subjects. Some may have experienced a particularly painful period in early family life, such as dealing with a parent who was alcoholic, and may have some trouble opening up. Others may have been conditioned by their upbringing to believe that it's in poor taste to talk about one's earnings or former love relationships.

Still, we suggest that you probe these closed-off areas and try to identify the reasons why your partner is reticent. The more you can open up with one another, even in the most secret or painful areas, the stronger your relationship is likely to be and the more opportunity there will be for healing change.

7. CAN SHE TRUST YOU?

Trust is really the bottom-line issue in any permanent love relationship. Things go wrong in every marriage, but the partners with the lowest risk of breaking up are able to overlook most minor mistakes and wrongs.

The healthiest, most trusting attitude goes something like this: "I'll trust you until you give me a good reason not to."

That's a motto that most people can live with. But not so the serious Suspicious Suitor. His credo may be stated more in these terms: "I don't trust anyone until he proves himself to me! You have to earn my trust."

The problem with this sort of person is that you can never win his trust. You may come through for him a hundred times during a relationship that has lasted for months or even years, but heaven help you if you slip up just once! Remember: The hard-core Suspicious Suitor *expects* to be exploited. Sooner or later, he'll find evidence to confirm his worst suspicions.

Helpless Me

The excessively dependent individual—what we've called the "Helpless Me" personality—is generally a rather likable sort. She will agree to almost anything, so long as there's no requirement to engage in hard decision making.

In general, dependent people try very hard to please others out of a fear of endangering important relationships or of being forced to rely on themselves. This "ready-to-please" quality has a certain attractiveness, particularly for "take-charge" partners who are more than happy to assume control.

Some typical exchanges between the Helpless Me and a stronger mate:

"Where shall we live?" asks the strong one. Answer: "You decide."

Or, "Where would you like to go on vacation?" Answer: "Anywhere you say."

Or, "What do you think?" Answer: "I don't know. How about you?"

The dependent character may be unsure what she would like to do, who she wants to invite to dinner, or even what she should wear. Some other traits that may be present in this person:

- He may be manipulative, not through normal guile but through a need for self-preservation. Illustration: "I have to talk her into going on this outing with me because I don't think I can handle all the required decisions by myself."
- She lacks self-confidence.
- He loves to put himself down, perhaps to the point of denigrating his intelligence or professional capabilities.
- She's morbidly frightened of responsibility.
- He doesn't mind being pitied or condescended to, so long as he gets the help he's looking for.

A number of questions were inserted in the Compatibility Quotient to identify the Helpless Me personality. These included items on the person's inclination to take charge of various situations, the capacity to make major decisions, the need to have one's own way, the readiness to back down during disagreements, the tendency to take risks, and the presence in the relationship of one domineering or "overwhelming" partner.

If two dependent individuals are involved in a relationship, they can often live together quite harmoniously, at least until a major calamity occurs. When that happens, neither person may be capable of making a decision or taking charge. The result may be a major crisis in the home, even a collapse of the relationship in the ensuing state of chaos and anxiety.

When there is one controlling partner and one dependent one, the couple may be better equipped to deal with the common problems of life, so long as there is an agreeable division of labor. In other words, one may make all the decisions and do all the planning, while the other acts as the "worker" or "gofer" in carrying out those decisions and plans.

Still, there are inherent weaknesses in this sort of arrangement.

We've treated quite a few cases of "strong-weak" marriages where the peculiar relationship has precipitated a major emergency, such as a financial crisis. In such circumstances, the weak one may find she "just can't cope," while the strong one becomes furious that his spouse can't be relied upon. This dissatisfaction may destabilize the marriage to the point that it self-destructs.

The Sad Story of Strong Tony and Weak Linda

Tony was a hotshot business executive who met Linda on a trip to Georgia. Charmed by her good looks and "Southern belle" gentility, he immediately fell in love with her. For her part, Linda thought Tony was the strongest, most decisive man she had ever met—and she had a long-standing predilection for strong men.

After a whirlwind courtship, they got married, and their first few years together were quite delightful. Tony made more than enough money to support his wife in style, and Linda loved to be supported and play the role of traditional housewife. Linda never pretended to have ambitions for a career outside the home. She was completely noncompetitive with her husband and was quite content to let him have the limelight.

From the outside, these two appeared to be perfectly matched: Linda loved to be coddled and taken care of; Tony loved to be the shining knight and hero of his home. On a deeper level, she also wanted a father figure, and he needed what amounted to a one-woman admiration society.

As Tony's business grew, he started to take big financial risks, and that was the point when things began to get more rocky in their relationship. Linda didn't like risk taking; chancy ventures made her extremely nervous. Feeling that their financial security might be threatened, she said on more than one occasion to her husband, "I'd really prefer to pull back on our lifestyle a little, save more money, and be more financially conservative."

But Tony was in charge, and he made the decision to keep pushing in his work and his investments. Unfortunately, he finally spread himself too thin, and one by one, his investments and business ventures started to go sour. He eventually got into debt far beyond his ability to repay, and he panicked.

For the first time in his life, he began to question his abilities and to experience anxiety attacks. In the past he had always slipped easily into the role of caring for and directing others, especially his wife. Now, he desperately needed Linda's understanding and help.

Linda, given her Helpless Me personality, was completely unable to respond or even be supportive. She never got to the point of saying, "I told you so." She became so paralyzed with fear that she couldn't think straight. For days on end, she would just loll in bed and weep.

"Come on, Linda, pull yourself together!" Tony would shout. "I know things are bad, but at least nobody's died. We can make it again. We can get back on our feet. But I can't do it alone. I need your help. I don't have anyone else to talk to. If I have to worry about you and be your emotional crutch, we're sure to go down the tube!"

"I can't, I can't," Linda replied, until finally Tony gave up on her and began confiding in one of the single women who worked for him in one of his businesses. Eventually, these conversations turned into an affair.

Tony's "line" to his new woman friend, though old and common, was quite true: "My wife doesn't understand me," he complained.

Surprisingly, though, Linda started to show even more resilience than she had thought she possessed. After receiving some strong advice and urging from her friends, she began to pull herself out of bed every morning to look for a job. Before long, she found an excellent position as a sales representative, and that was her first step in escaping both from her pressing anxiety about family finances and from her Helpless Me personality.

Having discovered that she had a knack for selling, Linda soon was bringing home sizable checks. The job also provided her with a new, firmer sense of her own identity and a growing self-confidence.

Still, the commuting and other demands of the job took their toll. She sometimes came home feeling tired and frustrated with her husband for what she now perceived were his business inadequacies.

Gradually, Linda began to criticize Tony for his mistakes. On a couple of occasions, when the arguments became quite heated, she blamed him for "losing all our money in those stupid speculative schemes."

Eventually, Tony's businesses recovered somewhat, but the marriage didn't. For one thing, he felt that his wife had let him down when he had needed her the most. Also, his ego had been sorely wounded by her criticisms. And he was miffed that she no longer looked up to him and depended on him as much as he required.

Tony continued with his extramarital affairs and eventually fell in love with a "sweet young thing" who was a replica of what Linda had once been. Before long, Linda and Tony were divorced, but soon, they were both repeating the patterns of their original relationship with new people.

Tony got married to his young companion and began to pamper her and dominate her as he had done initially with Linda. Linda became involved with her boss, a sales supervisor, and harbored the hope that he would eventually marry her, support her and allow her to go into permanent retirement.

Obviously, the story of Tony and Linda isn't a success story. What might they have done to head off the destruction of their marriage?

First of all, if they had been aware of their Compatibility Quotient, they might not have gotten involved with one another at all. Among other things, Linda's need to be treated like a child and Tony's desire to control would have been reflected numerous times in their answers, with a resulting low CQ for their relationship. On the other hand, if they had moved toward marriage, they might have been able to guard against the particular risks they faced because of the "strong-weak" configuration of their relationship. Linda at least showed the capacity for change when she was under fire, and if that transformation could have been effected while the marriage was still intact, this couple might still have been together.

Other partners we've counseled have taken steps like these, which might also have been helpful for Tony and Linda:

- The strong person helps nurture the self-confidence and independence of the weak one, the Helpless Me.

One strong woman who married a rather dependent, indecisive man constantly worked at building up her husband's self-esteem. She frequently complimented him on his strengths and encouraged him to take the lead in making family decisions. Furthermore, when it seemed that he was being pushed around by stronger personalities at work, she advised him to become more assertive and aggressive.

Like a parental surrogate, this wife succeeded in helping her Helpless Me husband to develop inner strengths, including an ability to stand up for himself and his beliefs, even in the face of strong opposition. He never became as dominant or powerful as many naturally aggressive men, but his improvements did manage to correct the imbalances in his relationship with his wife and to strengthen his position while at work.

- The Helpless Me may recognize that he must avoid becoming complacent or assuming a completely subordinate, submissive or passive role.

For example, one man felt incapable of handling any of the family's financial decisions because he felt his skills in this area would compare poorly with his wife's superior math aptitude. Yet he was determined not to remain an inactive or inadequate presence in this area of household responsibility.

He resolved to do some "on-the-job training" at home by taking on a few money management responsibilities. In particular, he began to think through and make firm decisions about his family's insurance needs, even though he had abdicated this responsibility to his wife. Then, having conquered the insurance question, he started to explore how he might help with the family investments.

With this step-by-step strategy, this husband, as well as other Helpless Me's whom we've observed, began to overcome his dependency. The result: The marriage became much stronger and more viable.

The Impact of Divorce on the Strong-Weak Relationship

Although the strong-weak arrangement may be relatively durable on the short haul, it frequently breaks down later on. As initial romance and sexual attraction become less important, the strong personality often wearies of continually bailing out the weak one. The strong partner may complain that he has outgrown his mate and may become restless for a change. At this point, disillusionment and infidelity become more common.

The issue here is not simply that one partner has outgrown the other, but rather that the ability of the two to interact effectively has failed. In the past, the strong partner may have found satisfaction in coming to the rescue. Now, she is sick and tired of that game; she wishes that Helpless Me would stop acting like a child.

The end result may be separation or divorce, and the weaker party often panics at this prospect. Faced with the possibility of a split, she may cling to her stronger mate even more tenaciously and accentuate those very passive qualities that are driving him away. More often than not, this vicious cycle ends in divorce.

Oddly enough, divorce may actually turn into a growth experience for the overly dependent person. Even stranger, the stronger partner is frequently the one who goes to pieces, as he realizes for the first time how accustomed he has become to taking care of the dependent spouse and receiving adoration from her.

In contrast, Helpless Me, finally forced to rely on her own wits, may gradually gain strength. No longer protected by an authoritarian, controlling parent-figure, she begins to realize that she is neither helpless nor stupid. She starts to shed that helpless image and role.

After divorce, many dependent men find they advance further at work because they can no longer count on their wife's income. They may even become more competent fathers as they find they have to make their own decisions with regard to their children. (On the other hand, dependent men who get divorced may avoid any contact at all with their children because they fear contacts with their strong ex-wives.)

Dependent women who undergo this transformation through divorce frequently discover that they have hidden talents. In general, they may become more independent and forceful as they are required to set up their own household and engage in dealings with others in the outside world. They soon learn, as one single woman in this situation said to us, "No one takes care of you but you."

Of course, we don't want to suggest that divorce is the best answer for those involved in a strong-weak marriage. In fact, if both partners recognize their personal quirks and the traps that may lie in store for them, they can take action to improve their chances of avoiding divorce. For that matter, unmarried couples may also be able to overcome the difficulties associated with the Helpless Me syndrome. Divorce, then, is usually a last resort for strengthening the naturally weak character.

The Sulker Variation

A common variation on the Helpless Me theme is the Sulker. Also known as the passive-aggressive personality, this person is characterized by dependence, but isn't nearly as pliant as the Helpless Me. The Sulker's basic dependency surfaces in angry sulking, not in helpless whining. He pouts and sulks when he doesn't get his own way. Still, he has virtually no self-confidence.

Passive-aggressive behavior often adapts amazingly well to a variety of difficult situations, especially where the power in the relationship is grossly unequal. The army private, for example, can't openly tell off his captain or he'll be court-martialed. If he wants to protest at all, he can do so only in passive ways, such as procrastination, inefficiency or forgetfulness. Although he can't disobey a direct order, there's no law that says he has to do the job well.

Sulkers may not display any openly hostile emotions, but make no mistake, that sulkiness is always present in some way. These people are hard to live with because they're chronically resentful about everyday demands.

An analogy to the Sulker's situation may be taken from the labor movement. Sulkers respond to demands not by a confrontational, home-based version of labor's picket lines. Rather, they engage in what amounts to household slowdowns or corporate sabotage. They work badly and slowly, demonstrating in this fashion that they are angry and discontented.

Common ploys of the Sulker and his relatives that we've heard related in our offices:

- "I know you asked me to bring home the tomatoes, but I forgot."
- "Stop harping on me. I'll do it later."
- "I'll definitely do it today"—but "it" doesn't get done.

The passive-aggressive character doesn't directly complain that he feels overwhelmed. Instead, he dawdles until his partner takes over and completes the task. The more active partner often remains chronically frustrated, not quite knowing where or how to assign blame. Also, the victimized spouse may begin to hate herself for becoming a nag and may end up doing most of the work in the home because it's easier that way.

Bad moods, notably sullenness, frequently grip the Sulker. And sullenness, which is a trait associated with all types of dependent people, makes for an extremely risky marriage. A typical interchange that one wife reported to us involving her sullen husband, Frank:

"How would you like to go out to a movie, Frank?" she asked.

"Nothing good playing."

"How about a restaurant for dinner? That would be fun for a change, don't you think?"

"Too much trouble."

"Well, how about a walk?"

"Nope."

"Why not?"

"Don't feel like it."

Sullen people pout and brood a lot. If they respond at all, it will probably be in monosyllables or short bursts of words, with the eyes averted.

They dwell on past slights and tend to forget those things that made them happy. Many times, they sink into bad moods for no apparent reason; they just seem to *need* to spend some time in a funk. A black cloud seems to follow them around more often than other people.

To put it bluntly, sullen people are killjoys. They seem happy only when others are as glum as they are. Moreover, they are remarkably skillful at spreading glumness wherever they go. They especially like to have others try—and fail—to cheer them up.

Without exception, sullen killjoys are hard to live with. Those who find some perverse satisfaction in being miserable or making those around them unhappy have a low Compatibility Quotient. Furthermore, if your potential spouse is a killjoy, your mutual Compatibility Quotient will be low. Despite the old adage that misery loves company, two sullen people are a lethal combination.

If you're involved with a partner who seems overly dependent, or perhaps has some sulky or sullen traits, there is hope. The challenge is to help your loved one overcome his or her dependency and gain more of a sense of independence, assertiveness and self-confidence.

How to Evaluate and Help a Dependent Person

There are some times when married partners must turn to others outside their relationship for help. But there are many other times when spouses should be able to count on each other to make decisions or provide support during a crisis. Hence, the importance of identifying the Helpless Me personality early and then either working to correct it or, if necessary and possible, severing the relationship.

To assist you, we've formulated a list of questions that you can use as a checklist to identify, evaluate and help the Helpless Me or Sulker in your midst.

1. DOES SHE SHOW INITIATIVE?

Initiative may be indicated by such habits as

- Starting projects on her own
- Making major life decisions, such as career choices, religious commitments or moral judgments
- Dealing with the petty problems of everyday life

It's fine if your husband respects your eye for color and asks which tie you think he ought to wear. But if he also regularly queries you about which shirt, which suit and which set of underwear, that's a tip-off to the Helpless Me personality.

2. DOES HE LACK SELF-CONFIDENCE?

A lack of self-confidence almost always accompanies the dependent personality. Helpless Me puts himself down constantly in an effort to seek protection or ward off criticism from others.

So ask yourself, "Does she ever stand up for herself, particularly when she's absolutely in the right? Can he tell you when you are stepping on his toes? Is she everybody's doormat?"

3. IS SHE A "NERVOUS NELLIE"?

Here are some typical exclamations you may hear from the overly dependent person:

- "Oh, no, the car engine's making noise. I think it's going to explode!"

- "The electric bill is five days late. Do you think they're going to shut off the lights?"
- "I get so worried about my checking account. I just can't seem to balance the checkbook. I'd ask for help at the bank, but they always make me wait or give me the runaround. Do you suppose you could help me?"

The world often seems to be overwhelming for Helpless Me. Everything takes an enormous amount of effort. As a result, the dependent character seems frequently to be "strung out," at the "end of my rope," or exhausted, even when, by any objective standard, things don't seem all that bad.

4. CAN HE TOLERATE CRITICISM?

As incompetent as he may appear to be when on his own, the dependent person is quite capable of doing tasks so long as he's under close supervision. He might actually seek work that is demeaning or below his capabilities in order to avoid the risk of criticism.

In general, Helpless Me is easily hurt by disapproval and will go to great lengths to keep from being yelled at. In order to avoid an argument, he will seem to agree with people, even when he knows they are wrong.

5. DOES SHE PROCRASTINATE?

Does your partner always put things off until the last moment? Does she miss deadlines, then give you a hangdog look, as if to say, "There's nothing I could have done"? Does she avoid obligations, then claim she "forgot"?

If any of these points applies to your loved one, you may be dealing with the Sulker variation of the dependent personality. The Sulker can drive you absolutely crazy with her failed commitments. You may try to pin her down, but never with success. Yes, she should have done a certain thing, but no, she just "forgot." Anyone can forget, of course, but for the thousandth time?

6. DOES HE HAVE A BAD ATTITUDE?

The term "bad attitude" may cover a multitude of sins, but here are a few that occur with regularity among dependent people, especially Sulkers:

- A tendency to pout when asked to do something
- A work pace that often seems to move along at a rate that's just slow enough to irritate you
- A calculated intention to do seemingly innocent (passive-aggressive) things that make you respond with a slow burn

Try asking your partner to do something that he doesn't really want to do, but that is important to you. Does he usually become irritable or stubborn, rather than being ready to talk or work things out? Can he be counted on to complain that you're making unreasonable demands of him?

7. DOES SHE LIKE TO PUT DOWN OTHER PEOPLE?

The Sulker is filled with resentments, particularly against people in authority. One sign that you're dealing with a passive-aggressive personality is that she constantly complains about her boss, the bill collectors or her parents.

Unlike the paranoid Suspicious Suitor, however, the dependent person doesn't assume that authority figures are out to get her. Rather, she feels that they are oppressing her by demanding that she take more initiative and move beyond her excessively dependent role.

These seven key questions, along with your basic Compatibility Quotient, should help you determine whether or not you're dealing with a dependent person—either the classic Helpless Me or the Sulker variation. The more deeply ingrained the dependency patterns are in this person's personality, the harder it will be for him or her to change. Yet without change, any love relationship, marital or premarital, will be on shaky ground.

On the other hand, if the dependency patterns are rather mild, as they often are, a sensitive, encouraging partner can often be the catalyst for beneficial transformations. What's required is helping the dependent person to develop the initiative, self-confidence, positive attitude and other attributes that he or she lacks—and not to feel threatened by the growing sense of independence.

The Escapist

A desire to escape is a very bad reason to decide to marry. Yet there are plenty of Escapists who are either on the verge of marriage, or are already wed.

Even a marriage that might otherwise work will likely fail if either partner is motivated mainly by a need to flee from something—whether boredom, loneliness, poverty, a disappointing love affair, or some other unhappiness.

We sometimes become so focused on what we wish to flee from that we give little thought to what will take its place. Even convicts who dream of escape and freedom are often disappointed to learn what awaits them on the other side of the prison wall.

Nancy Breaks Out

Nancy came from the kind of family that nightmares are made of. Dad was a drunk, physically abusive at times, but mainly sullen and preoccupied.

Mom was truly mentally ill. "She's nuts," the neighbors often whispered. "Eccentric and a vile temper," the close relatives said, a bit more generously. Nancy's brother was retarded and lived at home. To complete the gloomy picture, there wasn't much money.

Nancy had a certain natural beauty, and those who knew said her mother had been quite pretty in her day. Also, Nancy possessed an unusually nimble mind. She breezed through high school and won a full scholarship to a good college in another state. She had to turn it down, though, because her parents wouldn't let her leave home. Instead, she enrolled in a local junior college.

"Too many responsibilities here to run away to some big university," they told her.

Then Nancy met Doug in her freshman year at the junior college. At first, he seemed to be the breath of fresh air that she needed. Doug came from a rather formal and proper family, but at least they didn't have any skeletons in their closets. In fact, Doug turned out to be just what he appeared to be: a very handsome, none-too-ambitious, reasonably intelligent, genuinely nice guy.

After they had dated for a few months, Doug asked Nancy to marry him and, after thinking it over, she accepted. She didn't think she loved him, but then again, she had never found anyone she could say she genuinely loved. Unquestionably, though, Doug offered Nancy a life far better than her present circumstances, which she so desperately wanted to escape.

Because the two came from different religious and ethnic backgrounds, they settled on a simple civil ceremony with only a scattering of relatives present. After the wedding, they moved from the West to the East Coast and rented a small but adequate apartment in a large city.

The marriage was a disappointment from the start. Doug was kind, sane and abstinent, a vast improvement over Nancy's family life. But he bored her to death.

She tried to love him and convince herself that they were right for each other. Eventually, her repeated rationalizations no longer sufficed. It didn't work to tell herself, "He's really very nice and maybe this is all there is to love." Or, "I like him, but I don't love him. Still, that's probably the way most marriages are."

Finally, she gave up trying to fool herself. After eighteen months Nancy told Doug that she wanted out, and he agreed, as always, with grace and dignity. Ironically, that very evening they made passionate love, and Nancy came closer to loving Doug than ever before. But she stuck by her decision to end the relationship.

Nancy tried living by herself, but she couldn't tolerate the loneliness. She compulsively searched for a new partner and found one soon enough in Stan, a young and very successful physician from a background similar to her own. Stan, who had himself been married for a few months many years before, was quite taken with her. But it was Nancy who pushed him into the marriage.

Within a few months of this new marriage, Nancy became restless again. Stan was always seeing patients, it seemed, always hustling to make more money, running about to this activity or that. Stan didn't drink, but he did have a temper. He could turn quite nasty when he thought he had been crossed.

When Nancy came to us for help, she admitted she no longer loved Stan. In fact, she didn't even like him and preferred to call it quits. She had decided, though, to wait, have a child and perhaps through parenthood to turn her marriage around.

We recognized immediately that she was bound to fail. For that matter, she'll probably continue to fail as long as she keeps running away from her relationships. In short, she's the consummate Escapist.

You'll recall the pattern: Nancy first fled from an unhappy home into her first marriage with Doug. After becoming bored with him, she escaped once more but became lonely. Finally, she ended up fleeing into the arms of Stan, whom she now regards as a dud. She plans to escape again by having a child.

As we've worked with Nancy, we have focused a great deal on the issue of what motivates her, what causes her always to want to run away.

Why Are You Running Away?

Nancy must understand that she is running away from making a commitment. She is fleeing her deep-seated fears of intimacy. In the end, she is running from the pain of facing herself and dealing with her real needs. For the Escapist, relationships are compensation or reparation for the feeling of having been cheated earlier in life. Our response to Nancy, as well as to other Escapists, goes something like this:

Marriages rarely work if they are based on the need to escape. You may pretend to yourself that you love him or that she meets most of your requirements for a spouse. You may also convince yourself that you are attracted to a particular new person. But if you're *really* motivated by the need to flee from someone or something, your Compatibility Quotient will be dangerously low.

The simple truth is that you can't fool yourself, at least not for very long. You can't look that other person in the face and continue to tell yourself you love him if it isn't true. Sooner or later, you'll come to view him as an object or resent him. Before you know it, you'll be planning to escape once again.

A better approach: If you're not certain why you want to marry, then wait. After you've had time to think it over, you may not marry that person because you discover that you no longer need him to do for you what you cannot do for yourself. On the other hand, if you do survive as a couple after you've taken some time off, your Compatibility Quotient may become high enough to make a marriage work.

Furthermore, you should elect to postpone your decision to have a child if the only reason you want to do so is to escape from some problem or dissatisfaction with your mate. A new baby puts considerable strain on any marriage, and a relationship that is inherently weak will probably crumble under the pressure. Work out your problems with Escapism first. Then consider expanding your family.

Marriage on the Rebound

A particularly dangerous version of Escapism, one that is tailor-made to lower the CQ, is to marry on the rebound.

There are several kinds of rebound marriages. The most obvious is to become involved with a partner soon after the breakup of another important relationship in your life. The more significant the first relationship, the more risky the second, and the more likely it is that the replacement person is just an object to help you compensate for an overwhelming loss.

Why Jenny Began Bouncing About

Jenny dated Matt for seven years before the two of them decided to get married. They had been in love since junior high school, where they had been classmates. Neither had ever dated anyone else.

Because they were so young, their parents had played a particularly important role in planning their lives. The two families were neighbors and had always gotten along well. They all agreed that the wedding would be scheduled for the summer after the couple's freshman year at college. For a while, Jenny and Matt thought they had their life plans cast in concrete, with the prospect of living happily ever after firmly in their grasp.

Then Matt met Doreen in English class. He fell wildly in love with this willowy blonde, who seemed far more exotic than Jenny. Matt knew instantly that the old relationship was over, but he couldn't face Jenny and break the news to her.

It didn't take long for Jenny to catch on, however. Their sexual relationship evaporated, and Matt started leaving hints all over the place. He somehow began to be tied up on Saturday nights, which had been their main date night. Also, when Jenny got into his car, she was sure she caught the whiff of strange perfume on several occasions.

When Jenny finally confronted him, Matt confessed immediately, with considerable relief. It hadn't been easy leading a double life. Their engagement was officially broken, and the wedding plans were called off. Predictably, there was a great deal of unpleasantness that arose between the two families, but Matt didn't care; he just wanted out.

After the breakup, Jenny wept a good deal and began to cut classes. Within a week, however, she met Len, a rather shy mathematics major who had absolutely no experience with girls. Jenny overwhelmed him with her attentions and introduced him for the first time to the subtleties of dating.

Flattered to be the object of such affection from what he perceived as a very attractive and sophisticated young woman, Len embarked for the first time in his life upon a whirlwind social life. As for Jenny, she made little attempt to get to know him well as a person, or to meet his friends or family. She was mainly interested in having a serious boyfriend. She even began to insist that it was time they considered getting married.

Fortunately for both of them, Len had the good sense to question the speed at which Jenny was moving. Then, when she began to push him even harder, he pulled out of the relationship.

Jenny came to us for consultation at this point, and we advised her to wait at least a year before becoming seriously involved again. We've found that someone like this young woman, who has experienced severe emotional trauma as a result of a broken love affair, needs at least a year to allow inner healing to occur. Bouncing from relationship to relationship is a poor way to repair wounded self-esteem.

How might the Escapist respond to nonromantic losses in his life? People may marry on the rebound from practically any kind of loss, not just from a failed relationship. Yet the results can be just as disastrous.

One young man we saw insisted on marrying his long-time girlfriend just after he had been fired from his job. His unconscious reasoning went like this: "I've just lost something very valuable to me. Perhaps I can make it up to myself by treating myself to a wife. Also, I'd better act now because with the way the rest of my life is falling apart, I may not be able to find a decent wife!"

It may seem obvious that getting married isn't a good idea if you make the move at the very moment when you can least afford it or when you're least able to handle such a commitment. Historically, marriages that begin at times of crisis often don't survive, and most people, in their calmer and saner moments, are aware of this. But when panic sets in, reason may go out the window.

It's important for those who are vulnerable to the Escapist way of thinking to establish firm personal policies that protect them well in advance of any crisis from fleeing or rebounding. For example, we've given a number of people this advice:

- Allow yourself time and space to grieve after a major loss. Let your close friends help you with this process.
- Before blaming others, figure out the part that *you* have played.
- Leave at least six months (sometimes a year) after a crisis before making important decisions.

Such personal policies are essential because the chances are that any marriage that begins with escapism will end in divorce.

Another common type of rebound marriage occurs just after widowhood. A variant on this theme happens when a man or woman feels impelled to find a mate after losing a parent, brother or sister. A spouse can't replace a member of your family, nor is a new mate a replacement for an old one.

If you marry on the rebound after a major loss, there's the danger of expecting your husband or wife to make up for the loss. The demands that flow from such an expectation will put enormous pressure on the marriage. For example, the new person is expected to fill overwhelming needs: "You be what I need you to be, not who you really are." The Escapist often wants the new companion to relate to her as a doll relates to a child, as just an extension of the Escapist's needs. That's why we say that it takes at least a year or two to recover after a major catastrophe in your life.

The same holds true if you are contemplating a relationship with a person who has just sustained a major loss. Our advice: Move *very* cautiously. That man or woman has been wounded too recently to be able to make any kind of commitment.

If you think you really want to be involved with a person who has suffered a loss, you should be patient and understanding. You have to help your wounded friend to heal. Assure him that you intend to stick around to be a friend, but don't make any promises or long-term commitments until he's out of the woods.

To sum up: The minimum waiting time before considering a serious relationship must be at least twelve months following an important loss. And two years is probably a better rule of thumb.

The Trapeze Act Variation

Unlike those on the rebound, some people attempt to escape from unhappy relationships by seeking a replacement lover or spouse— in many cases before they even break off with the first person. We call this the "trapeze act," and those who engage in this trick are known as Trapeze Artists.

The Trapeze Artist specializes in handing herself off from partner to partner, rather than risk being stuck in midair, without any love relationship at all. But like real trapeze artists without a net, these problem personalities usually run into disaster in their relationships, as do those who marry them.

There are two main types of Trapeze Artist. The most common involves the man or woman who simply can't contemplate going it alone. This individual is terrified of loneliness. As soon as one relationship ends, or is even in danger of ending, this person looks for another ready handoff into a new relationship. The new partner may be only second-rate as far as the Artist is concerned, but second-rate is better than nothing.

The second type of Trapeze Artist is characterized by restlessness. Many people just can't stay in one place for very long. They are driven by a constant need for change and newness. They leave relationships not because they are dissatisfied with the person, but rather because they are bored. These restless Trapeze Artists are also frightened of commitments. The *quest* is the important thing for them, not the relationship. The promise of intimacy is thrilling, but actual intimacy has always been a painful experience.

How does the Trapeze Artist stack up with the Compatibility Quotient? The first type of Trapeze Artist, the insecure person, is a better bet in a relationship than the restless person. We've had a good deal of success in helping insecure men and women gain self-confidence, but helping restless people settle down is much more difficult.

Evaluating the Escapism in Your Life

We often advise Escapists to step back and try to get an overview of their lives during the past five years. To this end, we suggest this sort of informal analysis:

Look for any dominant patterns in your relationships. Do you see any tendency you have to escape or perform as a Trapeze Artist? If so, try evaluating your present relationship in light of this pattern. For example, if you marry Dick to get away from Tom, how do you know you won't soon be looking at Harry to escape from Dick?

To put this another way, you may think you love the new person that has appeared in your life. But it's important first of all to work out things with the old person and also to understand exactly where you've been going with your relationships. Here are some guidelines we urge people to follow:

- If possible, resolve problems with old or existing relationships before you get into a new one.
- Try to understand why your previous relationship has foundered.
- Accept your share of the responsibility for what went wrong and try to learn from your mistakes.

If you don't have a problem with Escapism but you think your present partner does, ask yourself these questions:

- Has he ever sustained a meaningful relationship that lasted more than a year?
- Has she demonstrated an ability to stick it out through crises?
- Does he always blame the other people in his life, or is he willing to accept some degree of responsibility for failure?
- What is her pattern of behavior after a major relationship ends? Does she invariably start a new one, or is she able to live alone?

The answers to these questions should provide you with some firm indication about whether or not you're involved with an Escapist. In any event, the person should have some track record of stability in relationships and demonstrate a willingness to work on problems. Your partner should also be able to accept a fair share of the blame for his failed relationships. Finally, he should be able to live alone without falling apart.

The Role of the Rescue Fantasy in Escapism

The need to escape is usually based on a rescue fantasy, which works something like this:

You feel dissatisfied with your life. You don't know exactly what's wrong, but you feel as if you are stuck in a rut. So you look for someone to rescue you.

Everyone goes through this process to some degree. Imagine you are a college freshman, struggling through a basic English course. Many years and many courses separate you from your degree. You start to daydream about marrying a millionaire, who will provide you with servants by the dozen, luxury cars and country homes. Then you come back to reality. You realize you may eventually achieve your goal, but it will take lots of time and hard work.

It's fine to have such fantasies, which after all, are nothing more than normal daydreams. Fantasy provides a psychologically healthy safety valve for our daily frustrations. If you try to act out the daydreams, however, such as by seeking a spouse to be your savior, you're asking for big trouble.

In the last analysis, if you say you want to marry but you really just want to escape, you are clinging to the childlike hope that your husband or your wife will make everything all right. By refusing to take responsibility for yourself, you are placing an impossible burden on the shoulders of your partner. Salvation through love is fine for fiction, but such rescues rarely take place in real life.

If you enter into a relationship because you feel you've met the perfect rescuer, the relationship will probably fail. Your partner will come to resent you for demanding more than he can deliver and, perhaps in the end, for making him feel useless and impotent. At the same time, you will come to resent him for disappointing you again and again.

A Final Note on the Escapist's Converse: The Avoider

The other side of the coin to escapism is avoidance. The Avoider is an individual who doesn't merely flee from relationships; he avoids them altogether. This person has a lifelong pattern of timidity and social problems.

You can identify the Avoider because he is a loner. He genuinely prefers to be by himself. Also, he rarely has close friends and maintains only superficial relationships with coworkers.

It's not unusual for such an individual to live with parents well into middle age. He stays away from activities that involve a significant amount of interpersonal contact. Furthermore, he may be easily embarrassed and readily hurt by criticism.

As you might expect, the Avoider, like the Escapist, has a very low Compatibility Quotient. He's not likely to be interested in marriage, however, and so the chances are slim that he'll ever place himself in a situation to be a risk to someone else.

The Angry One

Among the most frightening experiences reported by newly married men and women is their first awareness of their spouse's capacity for anger.

Up until day one following the wedding, it's usually been a constant round of fun and dating, with both partners on their best behavior. After marriage, though, some previously controlled or hidden anger is bound to emerge. We've already dealt with some manifestations of anger in the Suspicious Suitor and a few of the other problem personalities, but much more remains to be said.

Anger is an ugly emotion, but it's also important to recognize and accept it as a very normal part of the human condition. Either the man or woman may be the Angry One, though men are more likely to display their rage physically than women. Partners in the best of marriages learn to accommodate to their mate's resentments and displays of anger, from mild annoyance to outright rage.

Still, anger can be more than merely unpleasant. In many cases, it becomes quite threatening, particularly if it's directed at you by someone who is close. At the deepest level, anger represents a primordial fear of parental abandonment. Since human infants are so helpless, we learn from the earliest months of life that we are completely dependent on those who care for us. Parental anger, no matter how benignly expressed, tells the infant that he must shape up, or Mommy or Daddy might ship him out.

Every marriage is in part a recapitulation of our earliest life experiences. To some extent, therefore, one's spouse is something like a parent. When he directs a thunderbolt of anger toward you, the implicit threat is that he might leave. We may each handle anger in different ways and with differing degrees of aplomb, but we invariably have some trouble with it because it threatens us at a profoundly primitive level.

How Does Your Partner Show Anger?

There is no such thing as a marriage free of anger. Two people cannot live together very long without getting on each other's nerves. So beware of potential mates who rarely show displays of temper.

Chances are that the very individual you've decided is the "perfect person" is actually seething below the surface. The issue, then, is not avoiding anger altogether, but looking for a mate who expresses angry feelings in a form that you can tolerate.

Some people, for example, are comfortable with cool discussions of the most enraging topics. Others have to yell and scream to get their feelings off their chests. Still others need to withdraw temporarily to nurse their wounded egos.

Marriages work best when both partners are compatible in their styles of dealing with anger and resentment. Yet not all "anger styles" are acceptable to everyone. Moreover, anger may be a danger sign that there's been a failure to understand how one or the other partner is responding or operating.

In any event, excessive rage can have a profound effect on the Compatibility Quotient, and physical displays of anger will almost surely wreck a marriage.

The Emotional Volcano

Natalie and Fred had been married for twenty years, but Natalie was ready to call it quits. A petite woman with a pretty smile and sunny disposition, she had become fed up with her husband.

Fred's parents were withholding, unhappy people. They demonstrated little interest in the lives of their children or their families. Fred remembered long stretches when his father stamped around the house in a smoldering rage, saying nothing for hours on end. Because of some now-forgotten slight that had annoyed the father, Fred's parents had not even come to his wedding.

Fred had been a well-behaved child and struck most people as classy and socially adept, at least on first impression. Natalie remembers her initial attraction to him because of the quiet strength he exuded. Yet she was completely unprepared for his first volcanic explosion soon after the wedding.

The precipitating incident was trivial, something to do with her failure to show up for an appointment on time. But what could not be forgotten was the way that Fred heaped his rage and insults on her. He barely talked to her for two days; then, without warning, everything returned to normal, at least as far as he was concerned.

These volcanic explosions took place every month or two and were always extremely painful for Natalie, though Fred never got physical with her. Typically, his anger seemed to assume a life of its own, completely unrelated to outside events. Most of the time, Fred was quite placid and congenial around the home. At other times, a minor provocation could cause him to erupt.

During these explosions, Fred and Natalie stopped talking. They couldn't stand to be together in the same room. Every form of contact ceased, with the sole exception of sex, which if anything became more thrilling. Fred seemed able to channel his rage into wild caressing and lovemaking, and after they were finished, he was usually in a much better mood.

Throughout their long marriage, Natalie repeatedly attempted to deal with the explosions, but nothing ever worked. Fred's rages might include the kids, the dog or anything else that was in his way. At length, Natalie realized that she was genuinely frightened of her husband, despite the fact that he had never struck her. Sadly, twenty years of life together hadn't alleviated these fears.

This marriage was always highly at risk. Yet it lasted for a long time, mainly because Natalie was willing to endure Fred's rages. She finally threw in the towel when her children left for college. The periodic bouts of anger were threatening to destroy her emotionally because the kids were no longer around to distract him. So she acted to protect herself.

Is there any way a marriage like this might survive? Although such relationships are risky from the start, there are a few possibilities:

- If the nonangry partner can shrug off the rages of the Volcano and not get emotionally involved, such a marriage may make it. But this takes a very strong and somewhat thick-skinned spouse who can "tune out" the tantrums and let them blow over.
- The angry partner might go into therapy early in the relationship and learn to put a cap on his anger.
- Some angry partners have learned to control their anger better after undergoing a religious conversion experience and maturing in the faith under the guidance of a spiritual community or mentor.
- Occasionally, marriages where partners take long vacations from one another can remove the pressure. Constant exposure to the daily stresses of married life seems to be a major factor in triggering the Volcano into action.

The Brooder

Howard never exploded. When he was upset, he would just go into a deep state of gloom, which might last days or even weeks. No amount of coaxing could lift the cloud that hung over him— at least not until he was good and ready to have it removed.

"Now, darling, you look upset," his bubbly wife, Felicia, would comment.

"Nope."

"Would you like a drink?"

"Nope."

"How about a big, thick steak?"

"Nope."

One day Felicia thought she would try to shock her husband out of his torpor. She unexpectedly arrived at his office, closed the door, took off all her clothes and practically attacked him.

"Not in the mood today," he responded and went back to his work.

The Brooder's game is to try to make you feel guilty and responsible for his inner distress. The best counter, then, is to refuse to take on this guilt and responsibility.

How did their marriage turn out? As it happened, Felicia and Howard were well matched. As a result, their marriage flourished, despite his angry moods.

The key was Felicia, who possessed a great deal of self-confidence and a naturally irrepressible disposition. She rarely felt guilty about anything, so she had little difficulty ignoring Howard's irrational provocations. When he lapsed into a brooding spell, she just shrugged her shoulders and left to do some shopping.

If Howard had married a less secure woman, his marriage might have ended long ago. Insecure people fall into guilt quite easily, and they generally need ongoing reassurance. Brooders, though, aggravate their insecure mates, making them feel even less secure and often driving them right out of the house.

If Howard had married another Brooder, or someone with volatile emotions, or someone who could not tolerate silence, the marriage probably would have failed. Another bad choice for a partner like Howard would have been a Yeller, whose characteristics we'll be exploring shortly. This person loves to rant and rave to resolve differences, but the Brooder won't scream back. So the Yeller is deprived of the stimulation he or she craves.

On the other hand, if you're already married to a Brooder, don't despair. Just take your cue from Felicia: Don't get overinvolved with your mate's brooding, and above all, don't take it personally. The problem isn't with you; it's with him.

The Complainer

Although some people won't allow themselves to reveal what's really bothering them, they have no difficulty in expressing anger about outside pressures and annoyances. This Complainer will moan endlessly about all manner of trivia, and his complaints may often seem to have a paranoid edge.

Some typical laments:

"The government isn't being run correctly."

"The country's spending too much on defense—or too little."

"The mayor stinks."

"Cars aren't being built like they used to be."

"They shouldn't allow those kids to play their radios in the street."

"Why doesn't someone do something about the potholes?"

Kvetch, kvetch, complain, complain. It isn't that the gripes don't have some merit, because they often do. But they're often not that important in the big picture of one's life, and also they come with such irritating frequency!

Despite all this bellyaching, the Complainer rarely tells you what is really on his mind. Rather, he expresses his anger indirectly. If he thinks you are spending too much, he'll complain about the national budget. If he doesn't like the way you're dressed, he'll make nasty comments about current fashions. You know he's angry, and you sense you have something to do with it, but you're never quite sure what he's getting at.

Sometimes the Complainer may actually attack you directly, and you think you know what's bothering him. Even this sort of frontal verbal assault, though, can be deceptive. If you probe, you may finally discover that the Complainer is really upset about something very different from what he states.

The most malignant kind of Complainer—the one with the lowest Compatibility Quotient—is the help-rejecting Complainer. This man or woman begs for help but then turns around and does the very opposite of what you advise him or her to do. The Help-Rejecter desperately beseeches your input, then ignores it or rejects it outright.

One key to recognizing the help-rejecting Complainer is the simple two-word phrase "Yes, but." We always advise, stay away from any one who says "Yes, but" more than twice in one evening!

Almost no one can get along with a help-rejecting Complainer for very long because involvement with such a person leads to a sense of powerlessness. He may tell you "yes," but he's really just using that word as a frontline defense to give him time to slam you with a rejection, which is introduced by that telltale "but." He's expressing anger, which has nothing to do with the substance of the conversation, by automatically rejecting your proposals or suggestions.

It quickly becomes evident that this sort of partner just wants to stay angry or deal with it in his own time and way, without any outside help. Yet such an isolated way of dealing with inner feelings and turmoil will inevitably block off the possibility of a deep, mutually giving marriage.

Suppose, for instance, that you try to respond to your complaining partner's distress by offering logical suggestions. You're probably dealing with a Complainer if you find you always get the same, infuriating response:

"I think you ought to ask your boss for a raise if you feel you deserve it."

"Yes, but he would say no."

"Do you think we should go to the mountains this year?"

"Yes, but it might be too cold."

"Would you be interested in the shore?"

"Yes, but I hear that the bugs are fierce."

"How about Europe?"

"Yes, but there are so many terrorist incidents on airplanes these days."

In short, there's no way to satisfy the help-rejecting Complainer. These are simply very angry people who feel driven to express their deep-seated anger by rejecting you and everyone else in the context of ongoing grumbling. The actual content of their complaints isn't very important. They get their satisfaction by keeping you involved as observers of their unhappiness, rather than as real partners who can contribute to beneficial change in their lives.

The Yeller

Yelling is nothing more or less than a time-honored form of communication. The way it's used and the impact it has on a love relationship often depends on the Yeller's age and background.

All infants yell because they don't know any other way to let you know they're in distress. Adults who still harbor characteristics of the child may shout and yell for much the same reason.

On the other hand, yelling may also be a part of mature adult behavior. Some cultures frown on yelling by adults, while others look upon it with favor. A Japanese executive, for example, would make a very poor impression in his homeland by yelling at a colleague. (The Japanese build in occasions for yelling and releasing pent-up feelings. It's okay in the Japanese tradition to save it up and yell your head off on New Year's to drive the evil spirits from the home.) On the other hand, there are cultures where strong emotions are always expected to be expressed strongly.

In general there's nothing wrong with yelling, unless it bothers somebody. If you like to shriek, simply look for a mate who also likes to shriek. Yelling can actually be fun as long as it's not one-sided and no one becomes frightened or intimidated.

On the other hand, someone who likes quiet communication should stay away from the Yeller. The Compatibility Quotient in such a match is very low. Marriages between Yellers and Whisperers are unpleasant and are usually quite brief.

The Fallout of Physical Violence

Everyone may be entitled to toss a dish a little harder than normal into the sink, or maybe punch a wall if the frustration becomes too much. But if your partner destroys a set of china or punches or slaps another person, that's different.

Neither men nor women have a monopoly on physical violence, but this expression of anger is usually peculiar to males. When we read in the newspapers about women stabbing their husbands to death, these acts of cataclysmic violence usually represent the final chapter in a long history of wife abuse. Certainly there are exceptions, but in general, women are rarely inclined to inflict significant physical harm on their men.

In some respects, as ugly and disturbing as it is to see, we're fortunate that domestic violence has finally come out of the closet. Wife abuse and child abuse are facts of life that we simply can't ignore. This tragedy cuts across every subculture and social class.

Two-Fisted Steve

Carol was the product of a broken home. Her father had been physically cruel to her, to her sisters and most violently, to her mother. Her mother had never complained but often had trouble accounting for her own blackened eyes.

Ironically enough, Carol married Steve, a man very similar to her father and in a number of ways even worse. Steve, a college graduate and accomplished salesperson, had just been released from jail after serving several weeks on an assault charge. Captivated by his suave, self-assured manner, Carol didn't consider questioning his stories about having been railroaded by the judge and by the system. Furthermore, she was intrigued by his deep sense of sadness and his undeniable good looks.

Their marriage went along surprisingly well for almost two years, but then their first child arrived. Steve became profoundly jealous of his infant daughter and accused Carol of spending more time with the baby than with him.

To his credit, Steve worked hard and provided the family with a good living. At the same time, he expected plenty of attention, and he was totally oblivious to the needs of his wife and child.

One day when he arrived home, he found the house dark because Carol had been out shopping with the baby. She apologized profusely and offered to prepare a cold snack. But Steve was already on edge because of some problems at work. He flew into a rage and started throwing dishes.

Carol made the mistake of arguing back, and matters quickly got out of hand. Steve finally struck her and knocked her down to the floor. Even then, he couldn't keep himself from hitting her and cursing. At length he stormed out and spent the evening at the local tavern.

The next day, Steve was filled with remorse. He bought Carol a giant bouquet of flowers and a necklace. Before long, they were in each other's arms, weeping and making up.

But the same thing happened two weeks later. The problems always centered on the baby, with Steve accusing Carol of neglecting him. This time, Steve struck Carol in the face and bruised her cheek. She wanted to go to the hospital emergency room, but he begged her not to.

"They'll ask questions and get us all into trouble," he said. Since he seemed more contrite than ever and swore it would never happen again, Carol agreed to doctor herself at home.

Unfortunately, the cycle kept repeating itself, with sporadic episodes of violence followed by sincere expressions of remorse and feelings of guilt. Carol always forgave her husband, perhaps because his behavior was not completely unfamiliar. His actions evoked vague memories of her own parents and the way they related to each other.

Then Carol asked Steve if she could take the child and visit her sister in California. A violent argument ensued about Steve's usual concerns over who was getting the most attention. This time, Steve lost control and slugged Carol so hard that her head lurched back against the radiator.

She started to bleed from her nose and became almost debilitated by a headache and dizziness. "That's it," she exclaimed.

"That's all I can take," and she said she was going to call the police.

Steve threatened to kill her if she did, but she called anyway. The police took Carol to the hospital, where x-rays revealed a small skull fracture, but they hesitated taking action both because Steve's denials were so convincing and also because they were reluctant to get involved in domestic quarrels.

Carol decided she shouldn't remain at home, however, and so she contacted a battered women's shelter for help. Penniless and feeling too bad to take care of herself or her child, she threw herself on the mercy of those who ran the shelter. Fortunately, the shelter operators immediately understood her problem and took her in. They had seen many "Carols" in their work, and they knew just what she needed to get back on her feet.

Among other things, they provided temporary financial assistance and a place for her and the child to stay. Also, they helped Carol with the legal hurdles she faced, including the securing of a court order to keep her husband away from her. As a kind of insurance policy, a social worker discovered that Steve was still on parole, and she threatened to have it revoked if he interfered.

Does this marriage have a chance of being restored? The chances are minimal. In fact, our advice to Carol is that she regard the relationship as terminated—that she shouldn't even consider a reconciliation because of the potential physical danger both to herself and her child.

Some guidelines we'd like you to keep in mind on this issue of domestic violence:

- If you're a guy and find you have trouble controlling your fists around the woman you claim to love, you should think long and hard before you consider marriage.

  Your Compatibility Quotient is now close to zero. Unless you can get professional help that will enable you to bring your dangerous impulses under control, you have little hope of building a successful relationship. If you do get married, the chances are very good that your marital interactions will be nasty, brutish and probably very short.

• If you're a woman and the man you think you want to marry lays a hand on you in anger—or even threatens to strike or rough you up—stop everything! This arrangement simply won't work.

Hitting girlfriends and wives is a disease, and one which can be fatal. You may protest, "He's sorry about it, and he always apologizes." But you can bet that he'll go on beating up on you because that's part of the illness. Men who batter women are always contrite and self-loathing, at least until the next time.

In addition to those who express their anger with violence, there are many angry people who refrain from physical abuse. These other kinds of anger, however, can just as easily place a relationship at serious risk.

The Self-Hater

The ancient sages knew that you must love yourself before you can expect others to love you. Yet some people don't love themselves very much; they regard themselves with either contempt or despair.

Ideally, self-love should be learned at a very early age. Furthermore, problems with self-love or self-regard can be repaired in adulthood only through painstaking effort. Because this problem is so deeply ingrained and hard to overcome, those who have trouble liking and accepting themselves may also be highly destructive in love relationships. One of the most common ways that low self-love is expressed is through anger.

Self-loathing is generally recognized among counselors as a form of anger, one in which the rage is not expressed to others but turned inward, toward oneself. This self-directed anger corrodes the inner being, as hydrochloric acid eats up the surface. But even though self-loathers are very angry people, they often come across initially as being clingy or generally depressed.

The Self-Hater may tell you how great you are, how much she needs you, and how appreciative she is of your concern about her unworthy problems. Yet there is always a dark underside to the

Self-Hater's profuse expressions of gratitude. These individuals are quite capable of turning nasty if a partner should dare to think about withdrawing his support. The inwardly turned anger may leak out, as it were, and poison the relationship.

Holly was an attractive thirty-two-year-old executive secretary who had never had a successful relationship with a man. She finally decided that the problem might be in *her* rather than in the men she was meeting, and so she came to us for a consultation.

The only child of a depression-ridden family, Holly had always been a good student, but she had never been particularly happy. Her father had died when she was fifteen, and her mother had remarried. But Mom grew increasingly despondent and eventually committed suicide. Holly began to wonder if perhaps she could have been responsible for her mother's death. As a result, she started to feel guilty that she had moved away to college just before her mother had shot herself.

Holly had dated frequently, but she always chose her boyfriends in a blatantly self-destructive manner. For example, she avoided other college students and sought instead to get involved with men who were essentially unavailable.

One yearlong affair with an older, married English professor dissolved when the man returned to his wife. Then, there followed a string of bisexual partners, a sadist and finally a Con Artist who lived off her allowance until the police forced him to leave the state.

Once in a while a nice guy did manage to get through to her. A few of them really liked her, but she always turned them off. If they showed any real interest, she became cruel and cutting until they went away. Invariably, she would explain that Joe or John or Jim just didn't meet her expectations.

To put this another way, Holly had a split view of men. Her ideal man didn't exist in flesh and blood, and that was the main reason all her potentially viable dates fell short. On the other hand, she readily fell prey to the most unsavory characters.

Holly has now begun to understand more about the self-loathing that has been driving her, and she's beginning to learn to deal with it. Among other things, she is more alert to the dangers she faces as a Self-Hater when she enters into a love relationship. She recognizes that she has been assuming she doesn't deserve nice guys, but only those who confirm her mistaken sense of unworthiness.

As for her current romantic situation, Holly has just become involved with a guy she says she really likes. But she's afraid that she will lose control of her emotions, and after a fit of self-hating, she'll drive him away. As a result, she has been in a frequent state of depression as this relationship has developed.

"What can I do to save this relationship?" she asked us. "What can I do to keep from sabotaging it?"

Our advice to Holly, which applies to other victims of angry partners, so far seems to be working quite well. It goes like this:

- You're far ahead of where you were just a year ago because now you recognize that you are a Self-Hater and you're committed to doing something about it.
- Your Compatibility Quotient is still rather low because you're wrestling with the residues of self-hate, but take heart. That CQ is steadily rising!
- Move along slowly in this relationship, and don't try to make any important decisions until your current depression has lifted. Chronic depression is a condition that needs professional care, and marriage is no cure for it.
- In fact, marriage in general often aggravates the problems resulting from low self-worth. For example, the more your spouse tries to give you love to counteract your poor self-image, the more guilty and unworthy you are likely to feel. Yet the more he pulls back, the more you'll become angry and start demanding his love and support. You'll be caught up in a vicious cycle that will produce rancor and alienation rather than love.
- You must continue to work hard at raising your self-esteem, independent of any love relationship. This implies approaching people more as an adult than as a child. You can't derive self-esteem from someone else, however loving and

patient that someone is. Conversely, your spouse can't obtain his sense of worth from you.

How do you increase your self-esteem and lower your self-hating?

There are many ways a person may work on raising self-esteem, and they all take time and effort. Here are just a few that we've found to be helpful:

- Make an objective evaluation of your strengths, talents, achievements and potential. Don't attach any "buts" to this list. Just jot down all the things that are good and impressive about yourself. Read the list as often as you can—at least twice a day.
- Put yourself in the company of positive people who build you up.
- Stay away from people who tear you down.
- If you're in a job where your boss or coworkers frequently dump on you, find another position with more supportive colleagues.
- Involve yourself with activities that are uplifting and that make you feel good about yourself. Inspirational or positive-thinking books can be a real help here.
- Find a mature friend, member of the clergy or therapist who can introduce you to practical personal applications of the concept of self-love and self-acceptance.

We expect that with this program as part of her life, along with some therapy to help with her earlier losses, Holly will soon be ready for a long-term love relationship. She has found that self-hate, while a formidable enemy to happiness, is nevertheless a foe that can be vanquished by those who are willing to replace their anger with self-esteem.

How Much Anger Is Too Much?

People differ greatly in the amount of anger that they are able to tolerate from another person in a love relationship. There are no fixed rules except one: Physical violence is *not* acceptable. Marriages don't work when people are being hurt.

So how much *verbal* anger or *passive* anger are you prepared to tolerate? To find this answer, ask yourself this series of questions:

1. DO DISPLAYS OF ANGER TEND TO MAKE YOU QUEASY?

Some people just can't tolerate negative feelings. Perhaps they grew up in homes that were ultracivilized. Just as likely, they may have been raised by parents who fought constantly. In the first case, they are unaccustomed to fighting; in the second, they are sick of it.

If you can't tolerate strong emotions, accept that fact about yourself and stay away from relationships with angry people, or those who are free in expressing their anger. There are plenty of other men and women who would be willing to share a peaceful lifestyle with you.

2. DO YOU CARRY A GRUDGE?

A marriage won't last for very long if both spouses carry grudges. It's all right for one spouse to be a pouter if the other is willing to put up with it and try to smooth things over. Suppose the husband gets angry and stops talking to the wife for a while. The wife responds by rubbing the husband's back and whispers softly into his ear until he comes around. Then, everything is harmonious once more.

This is a very common arrangement, and marriages based on it tend to be quite stable—just so long as the Angry One doesn't take his case to an extreme. One partner may simply *enjoy* getting angry every so often, and the other may find satisfaction in making everything happy again.

Beware, though, if neither of you is willing to take that first step toward reconciliation. In that case, your CQ can be very low.

3. IS ONE OF YOU DEPRESSED?

Depression is a variant of anger. Often defined as anger turned against the self, depression can be a quite normal emotion for most of us. There's usually no problem with occasional, short-term bouts of depression; our concern arises when it's severe or lasts for long periods of time.

Severe depression can destroy an individual or a relationship if it goes untreated. Professional intervention, on the other hand, which sometimes includes the prescription of antidepressant medications, can result in successful treatment of serious depression, so long as the problem is caught in time.

Our advice in a nutshell: If you're unmarried, get to know your partner well enough to tell whether she seems to have normal, mild bouts of depression or the more serious, self-destructive kind. If the former, your CQ probably won't be affected much; if the latter, it probably would be best to guide the person to a qualified therapist or physician. In any event, be sure to avoid any deep or long-term romantic involvement until the problem has been dealt with successfully.

If you're married to a person with chronic depression, it's essential that you arrange for professional treatment as soon as possible. After all, you've made a permanent commitment to this mate through the matrimonial vows to stand by him "in sickness and in health." In this situation, you are dealing with a serious sickness that demands immediate intervention.

4. HOW CLOSELY MATCHED ARE YOUR "ANGER STYLES"?

Consider for a moment how well you and your partner are suited to one another emotionally, especially in the way you express anger. A few guidelines:

Two people may be able to yell and scream, then make up and get along quite well. Others, though, may find they have to discuss their differences with delicacy and restraint. Still other individuals become upset by hot outbursts of anger, while another group may be more affected by cold rage.

The problems with partners' "anger styles" arise when their manners of expression don't mesh. In many cases, these styles may reflect differences in cultural or family background, as well as varying life experiences.

It's worth comparing your background with that of your partner to see if there's a basis for your different modes of expressing anger and other feelings. You may find you're misinterpreting the style your partner sometimes uses in responding to you: What may be considered normal yelling in your family could sound like homicidal rage in hers.

To evaluate your respective anger styles further, ask yourself questions like these:

- Does he scare you when he gets angry?
- How long does it take for the two of you to make up?
- Can you calm each other down fairly easily?
- Does he give you the silent treatment, and if so, can you tolerate it?

The key to evaluating the anger in your relationship is not so much the absolute quantity of the anger as the successful matching of your means of expressing it. So, compare and evaluate your different anger styles with an eye to determining what you think you can take over the long haul in a relationship, and what you can't take. If you find that your anger styles mesh rather well, then your Compatibility Quotient is likely to be much higher than if the expression of anger drives wedges between you.

TEN

The Lazy Bones
and The Work Addict

Everyone knows that a certain amount of industriousness is essential to a viable marriage. Someone has to work, someone has to care for the kids, and someone has to keep the house. The economic and social pressures in today's world require a sharing of effort and responsibility in the strongest marriages.

On the other hand, it's necessary for couples to strike a balance between work and leisure. Too much work by one or both partners leaves little time to nurture the marriage relationship. Similarly, too little effort by one spouse may cause the other to feel overworked and resentful that the other isn't "pulling his load." This tension has led us to highlight the dangers of being either a Lazy Bones or a Work Addict in a marriage relationship.

What's Wrong with Being a Lazy Bones?

When one or both mates refuse to pull part of the load in the household, the marriage is automatically in trouble. Laziness is a complex problem and may be founded on one or more factors, like chronic depression or a sense of entitlement (e.g., "I deserve to relax a little after work!"). It may also be that the inert individual is just plain spoiled.

Whatever the cause, laziness or irresponsibility will drive down the Compatibility Quotient, and that's why we've included a number of items related to this topic in the CQ questionnaire. Yet the value placed on activity, in fact the very definition of activity as opposed to inactivity, is a relative issue that depends on each partner's personality and background, as well as on the outside economic and social pressures facing the family. Being "laid back" is not necessarily the same as being lazy.

Here are several illustrations showing how couples with different expectations and understandings of an optimum activity level may either get into trouble with laziness or actually make excellent use of their extra free time.

One couple found they were mismatched in the sense that the husband put an emphasis on devoting the entire weekend and most weekday nights to family activities, while the wife didn't.

He loved to play with the children, take walks in the nearby woods, pursue hobbies and in general just relax. This man liked to live for the present and enjoy his life *now*, rather than working to save for what he saw as an uncertain future.

His wife was just the opposite. She held down a demanding job, which required her to work frequently on weekends and late at night. She also supervised the child care services during the day. Finally, she set and worked hard toward personal financial goals that would pay for private schools for the children, for tennis lessons, for expensive foreign vacations, and for an extremely comfortable retirement.

In the view of this wife, the husband was a Lazy Bones. She thought he was being irresponsible in failing to place a high priority on preparing for the future. As for the husband, he felt increasingly under pressure from his spouse because of his laid-back work habits.

When this couple came in for counseling after a series of hot arguments on this subject, we helped them sort through their different values and goals in life. For the first time, they came to understand that they both wanted approximately the same things; they just had chosen different ways of trying to achieve their objectives.

The husband saw that the wife was as interested in the welfare of the children and the happiness of the family as he was. She just expressed her love and concern in a different way. In fact, he acknowledged that he had been a little too relaxed and remiss in upholding his responsibilities of managing the household and overseeing the activities of the children.

The wife, for her part, saw that she needed to pull back on her hard-driving approach to work and her single-minded goal of accumulating money for the future.

"After all, there may not be a future!" she finally admitted. "We may only have a year or five years together, and then one of us could die, or some other tragedy might occur."

This insight enabled her to place a greater priority on living for the moment instead of living exclusively for the future. On the other hand, her natural propensity to prepare to meet the children's college expenses and the couple's retirement needs influenced her husband to focus more on helping her in the work of family financial planning.

Another couple ran into fewer problems because, from the outset, they were more naturally suited to one another in their approaches to work and leisure. Both husband and wife were easygoing types who preferred their leisure time to material wealth. As a result, from the very beginning of their relationship, they had very high CQs.

Their work did not control them, and they naturally devoted a lot of time to each other and their children, even as they ignored the cultural pressure to accumulate wealth and maximize their career potential. They elected not to be envious of their neighbors, and when faced with the decision to work or play, they almost always chose to swim together or take a long weekend rather than work a second shift.

From the outside, these two might seem lackadaisical or even irresponsible. But outside opinion is not the important thing. The key consideration for their compatibility as a couple: Neither of these people is a Lazy Bones in the eyes of the other, and neither much cares about how they appear in the eyes of the world.

In general, though, those who are very interested in achieving high social standing and material comfort should stay away from a Lazy Bones. These people, though often quite likable, can be extremely frustrating when they get involved with someone who is achievement-oriented and ambitious.

If you yourself are a Lazy Bones, however, or affirm values that don't require upward career mobility and worldly accomplishment, then marrying a Lazy Bones may be a good idea. One of the most contented couples that we've seen are a dentist and his wife, who doubles as his office receptionist. The pair work only three days a week, and they consider that a heavy load. They spend their copious free time studying country crafts like basket weaving, going camping, and working on their tennis and golf games.

But what about the opposite—the hard-driving husband or wife for whom work is a pleasure, even an addiction? Can workaholics make good spouses? Is it possible for a Work Addict to have a successful marriage with a less ambitious mate?

The Work Addict

Workaholism means more than long hours: It's a state of mind. Simply put, Work Addicts would rather work than play. They prefer their jobs to anything else in their lives. They continue to think about work even when they are supposedly enjoying leisure. Work gives them a way to feel competent and powerful, and at the same time to avoid close emotional relationships. They usually produce a great deal, and receive rich rewards in money and praise.

Work Addicts have enormous energy, all focused on their only interest: *work*. They are impatient with subordinates or friends or with a family member who may need to sleep or relax. In a classic tribute to workaholism, E. L. Klavans, the legendary Washington, D.C., builder, refused to hire any man who smoked a pipe. "With all that tamping and lighting and puffing," said Klavans, "he'll never get any work done."

Marilyn Machlowitz, a management psychologist, studied dozens of hard-driving and successful men and women ten years ago and arrived at some remarkable conclusions. True workaholics, by her estimate, constitute only 5 percent of the population. They are both successful and surprisingly happy. Intense and driven, they work long hours without feeling stressed. They love nothing more than what they do.

But any complete evaluation of the Work Addict must also take into account the impact of his obsession on those around him. It should come as no surprise that Work Addicts often make poor mates and awful parents. They're rarely home and hardly ever want to be. The reason: Their self-esteem is based on being accomplished, not being at home. Also, they don't accommodate to anyone else's schedule, and when they are around, they need to be in absolute control.

Furthermore, these addicts seem to have little need for intimacy, and even sex is not high on their list of priorities. As for spending time with kids, that's an obligation, not usually a compelling joy. The plain fact is that to the Work Addict, domestic life is a necessary bother; it just can't compare to the glamour and excitement of life on the run in the office.

Biff, a rising business star, met Lana on a trip to Italy. The daughter of an Italian aristocrat, Lana was an art student in Milan. She quickly fell in love with this darkly handsome American, who seemed full of boundless energy and fascinating ideas.

As an international representative for a construction company, Biff made frequent trips abroad. On weekends and evenings, he studied at home for two different master's degrees. Obviously, his schedule was overloaded. But he did make time to call Lana each time he went to Europe, and the two would typically meet on the Costa del Sol.

Their dates were brief and intense, as suited the schedule of a Work Addict. Biff seemed always to have to leave as soon as he arrived. But he exuded so much energy that Lana felt they had lived a full week in the space of just one day.

Biff proposed to her by phone from somewhere in Asia, and she immediately accepted. After their wedding, Lana moved into Biff's Los Angeles apartment, a nice enough place but one that Biff had used mainly to shave and change suitcases.

Lana was content at first. She had lots of free time to paint and draw, as she eagerly awaited Biff's next return. Their social engagements when they finally got together were always exciting and glamorous, even if the conversation usually turned to shop-talk.

Lana had gone into this marriage with her eyes open. She knew she had married a Work Addict, but her life seemed rather satisfying, and she didn't complain. Before long, Biff was promoted to manager, and he no longer had to travel. But his habits had already been formed. He still made little time for anything besides his work.

Then Lana decided she wanted a child. She thought that a son or daughter would keep Biff more involved at home and provide company for her when Biff was gone. She was wrong on both counts.

When their son was born, Biff made all the proper fatherly noises, but he had little real interest in another outside "project"— in this case, parenthood—which took him away from his work. In fact, he came home even less often because now there was too much noise in the apartment to read or write reports.

Children, Lana discovered, don't substitute for a mate. If anything, small children highlight a spouse's absence and fill the stay-at-home partner with resentment and despair.

From time to time, Lana suspected Biff of having a mistress. When she called him at work, however, he was always glued to his desk, even in the wee hours of the morning. He occasionally took his son to the zoo, but on those outings he usually dictated memos into a small recorder while the boy fed the elephants.

Biff once even sat bolt upright during sex when a particular marketing thought hit him. He immediately called his secretary to set up a meeting for the following day while his wife just leaned back on her pillow and shook her head.

Feeling bored and abandoned, Lana finally decided she had to begin to build a life apart from Biff. She found a baby-sitter and enrolled in a graduate business course. Biff, though, didn't notice.

Then, she took a lover and began to arrive home very late at night. Still, Biff didn't notice.

Finally, she left him and filed for divorce. This time, Biff did notice and he did care. Even though Lana was willing to try a reconciliation, Biff admitted that he was unable to provide her with what she really needed: his time and presence.

In the separation agreement, Biff was magnanimous in awarding his family generous financial support. He was so understanding that he told his friends, "If I were she, I would have left me long ago."

Many workaholic marriages end in divorce, and the workaholic's Compatibility Quotient is very low. Several members of Machlowitz's sample were surprised that their spouses stuck with them at all. She observed that "living a life of peaceful coexistence with a work addict is certainly not impossible, but [even] that minimum return will require plenty of patience and countless compromises—all on your part."

Should You Marry a Work Addict?

To answer this question, it's important to ascertain what kind of a person you are: Are you a Work Addict yourself, a Lazy Bones, or somewhere in between?

You can answer this question for yourself by evaluating just how important outside work, with its status and prestige, is for you. Check how much time you devote in a given day to your work and how much to your relationships. Obviously, this sort of evaluation is an individual thing. But if the situation seems unduly lopsided (e.g., one hour for relationships and twelve for work), you're probably in the addict category.

Two workaholics in a family fare better than one, particularly if they don't have children. They understand each other well and can support each other's needs and ambitions. They need not spend much time together, nor do they require a great deal of physical contact.

On the other hand, if you're not a Work Addict yourself, other considerations come into play. First of all, in most cases a Lazy Bones should never get involved with a Work Addict. Their respective systems of values and lifestyles are too divergent for them to hope for a successful marriage.

If you're more active and ambitious than a Lazy Bones but still not a Work Addict, you'll have a better chance at marital success. But you'll also want to keep a number of important considerations in mind.

On the positive side, many workaholics are in high-status positions and are exciting to be with—at least, when they're around. Moreover, they're usually sober, financially responsible and reasonably faithful. Work is their paramour; they need no other.

A Work Addict may not be so bad if you're a private person, or are used to doing things for yourself. The time alone and freedom from the demands of a constantly present second party may actually be a plus.

But there are also some negatives: You should think long and hard before marrying a Work Addict if you want to have children right away. If you're already married, you should have some serious conversations with your hard-working spouse before deciding on children, just to be sure that you both have a firm understanding on how responsibilities will be divided.

Some further questions to ask yourself if you're thinking about getting involved with a Work Addict:

- How important are money and status to you? If they are a top priority, a Work Addict may be just the thing. But an often-absent wife or husband may be a high price to pay for a life of financial ease and vicarious glory.
- How important is companionship? If you function best alone, then the workaholic may fit the bill. If you see marriage as a true partnership, one in which each spouse shares

responsibility and works together to build a homelife, then getting involved with a Work Addict may be unwise.

- How important is sex? If you crave physical touching and lots of intimacy, stay away from the Work Addict. You won't find enough romance with this person.

The Compatibility Quotient is highest when both partners are able to balance work and play in a similar fashion. If you love to work, find someone else who also loves work, or at least is willing to support you wholeheartedly in your labors. If you put a higher priority on your leisure time, choose a partner with a similar bent.

Above all, *keep talking* with each other about your current commitments and future aspirations. That way, even if you happen to be a little out of sync with one another at times, you can at least make midcourse adjustments that will enhance your compatibility.

The Substance Abuser

Many of us have minor addictions—to coffee, for example—but these behaviors don't dominate our lives. We are able to put our work and families first and control our habits if they are interfering with our lives or health.

For purposes of the Compatibility Quotient, minor addictions, which for medical purposes are usually not regarded as addictions at all, generally don't interfere with a love relationship or marriage. But major addictions, such as those involving alcohol, drugs or gambling, may seriously undercut anyone's CQ.

The distinction that separates the addict from the nonaddict is *control*. The key question to ask is, "Am I in command of my behavior, or is it in command of me?"

Some people, who seem to gravitate from one addiction to another, are often lumped into the general category of "addictive personality." Recent research strongly suggests an actual genetic defect in these individuals. They may start by abusing alcohol, then move to a variety of drugs, then become involved in gambling activities. It seems as if these individuals need to grab onto something to be able to feel good, to recover from some emotional wound, or just to calm down.

A true addict will always put his addiction first. If he's in a relationship, he may genuinely not want to lose you. At the same time, he's not prepared to sacrifice the substance or habit that makes him feel so good or gives him comfort and support. As a result, the addictive individual has great difficulty entering into intimate relationships.

It May All Begin with Alcohol

Alcohol is unquestionably the most common of the drugs that are likely to destroy a marriage. In fact, if we had to list the most important overall cause for marital failure, it probably would be alcoholism.

The problem, though, is much more complex than it first may appear. For example, there is still no universal agreement on a definition for alcoholism. Nor is there a consensus about where the border lies between normal alcohol consumption and problem drinking.

To compound the difficulty, the sale and drinking of beer, wine and liquor in any quantities are perfectly legal. Furthermore, at least half the American public drinks, and many would argue that drinking is a normal, even healthful activity. On the other hand, by the most conservative estimates, at least 5 percent of American adults are alcoholics, a figure that translates into some ten million people.

A few common signals emerge from those who work with problem drinkers. These include:

- The impairment of one's judgment or job performance
- Acts that jeopardize the health and safety of the drinker or the well-being of other people

- A pattern of binges, even if the binges occur only every few weeks or so
- A tendency to deny that there is a problem
- The damaging of important relationships, including marriage

What Alcohol May Do to a Marriage

In working with various alcoholics in love relationships, we've identified a number of recurrent themes:

Alcoholic women are most at risk for marital dissolution.

We've found that for the most part, men don't put up with alcoholic women very long, the Betty Ford and Kitty Dukakis stories notwithstanding. But even though sober men tend to dump their alcoholic wives, sober women as a group don't reject their husbands as readily.

The reason for this distinction between the sexes? The cause is not entirely clear, but one possibility is that in the view of many people, it's less socially acceptable for a woman to be an alcoholic than for a man.

Also, many women tend to be more patient and nurturing in difficult relationships than men. They may also have fewer options, especially if they have children. One long-suffering wife, in discussing her alcoholic husband, told us, "I know he's got a problem, but I really believe that with love and understanding he can conquer it." She stuck with him for years before she finally gave up.

In contrast, a less understanding husband summed up the feelings we've heard from many males when he complained, "I've got too many other things to worry about than to have to deal with Mary's drinking problem. She's just going to have to handle this herself."

The children of alcoholics tend to marry alcoholics.

It seems as if the more a person has suffered as a youngster under the hand of an alcoholic parent, the more likely he is to repeat the mistakes of his parents. Sigmund Freud called this self-defeating behavior the "repetition compulsion," the compulsive need to return to the scene of the crime, no matter how laden with danger and disappointment it may be.

Such a reaction may sound crazy, but that's how human nature often works, as Francine found out when she finally tried to enter into an adult love relationship.

Like Father, Like Husband

Francine's parents came from first-generation immigrant European families. Her mother was devoutly Roman Catholic and never touched a drop of alcohol. Her father, on the other hand, was a bartender who loved his work because it let him imbibe off and on, all day long.

Francine's father never missed a day of work. He was gregarious and always pleasant with the patrons at the tavern. But his spirits took a meaner turn when he came home, perhaps because he was tired of having to be nice all day.

Usually, he continued drinking after work and rarely did more than stare at the television set. Once in a while, after one of his drinking bouts, Francine's father would become enraged by some trifle. For example, dinner might be prepared a little late or a little early, or the kids might have been making too much noise. It didn't seem to matter.

When these moods struck him once or twice a month, he would start breaking things and striking out at everyone in sight. As we saw during our sessions with her, Francine still has scars on her arms to remind her of her father's wild assaults. But nothing hurt her more than watching her mother sit silently while her father cursed and spat.

Francine swore to stay away from alcohol and like her mother, she never drank. She promised to avoid entanglements with alcoholics, and vowed never to marry one—that is, until she met David.

Dave was a charming young guy from a background similar to hers, and he was quite familiar with the problems of drinking because his family included a couple of alcoholics too. Although he drank himself, he promised Francine that he wouldn't go overboard. He assured her that he could control his drinking: "After all, I know from my background what drinking is all about!"

When he turned up drunk after a few college parties, he amiably explained to Francine that these incidents were just a slip, and also, he wasn't the only one: "*Everyone* got carried away!"

Despite certain misgivings, Francine decided she would trust David. They got married right after college graduation. Unfortunately, however, the drinking didn't stop; instead, it got worse.

Dave generally remained good-humored, though he seemed to bristle whenever she made even indirect references to his excessive alcohol use. All Francine dared to say was, "Dave, do you think you may have been talking a little too loudly at that party?" or "Dave, I feel so lonely when you fall off to sleep so early."

In any case, the clear-cut issue of alcoholism stayed in the background.

As Dave's illness progressed, increasingly obvious signs emerged. He became more taciturn, sometimes saying nothing to Francine for weeks. When he did talk, he was often verbally abusive. All his problems became Francine's fault: "I was happy as a single man. Sometimes I wonder why I ever got married." At times, he hinted that there were many other women who could understand him better than his wife.

Dave eventually went through a series of jobs, each position lasting for a briefer time than the last. Also, he began to have accidents in the car and complained about vomiting blood.

Even more ominous, his temper tantrums became uglier, and he started striking her. Francine rationalized that this wasn't really physical abuse because she wasn't seriously injured and the blows rarely left any marks on her body. But she did feel humiliated, to be pushed and hit by her husband.

With increasing frequency, Francine thought about her long dead father. She decided it was ironic that like her mother, she also had ended up marrying an alcoholic.

But unlike her mother, she was determined to do something about the situation. She joined Al-Anon, the counterpart to Alcoholics Anonymous, which counsels spouses, relatives and friends of alcoholics.

As the situation stands now, Francine acknowledges that she still loves Dave and wants to salvage their marriage. She has made it clear to him, however, that she won't continue to live with him if he abuses her physically. He has agreed to this condition and is in the process of seeking medical help, but it's obvious he has a long way to go.

Will this marriage make it? There are good signs in that both Francine and David are trying to deal with their relationship and with the alcoholism through experienced outside assistance. Still, until Dave demonstrates an ability to control his alcoholic tendencies, the CQ for this marriage will remain quite low.

Of course, alcoholism is *not* limited to men. But the female version of the problem has often remained hidden or misunderstood. For years, for instance, the drinking patterns of alcoholic homemakers were hard to document both because of the great stigma attached to female closet drinking, and because these unhappy women never had to sober up in time to punch the time clock at some job.

As women have become the equal of men in the marketplace, they are gradually rivaling male performance in the barroom as well. The telltale signs are in the statistics: The rate of male alcoholism hasn't changed much over the past twenty-five years, but the incidence of problem drinking that has been clearly identified in women has skyrocketed to practically the same levels as that of men.

In any event, whether a man or woman is involved, excessive drinking can be devastating to a marriage.

How Can You Identify and Deal with Alcoholism in Your Love Relationship?

If there's a history of alcoholism in your family or your partner's, you should be extremely cautious about marriage. Furthermore, if you or your partner had both parents who were heavy drinkers, the risk of alcoholic divorce is immense.

How can you identify the degree of danger—and perhaps deal effectively with it?

The line between normal drinking and alcoholism may not always be so clear. The quantity of alcohol consumed is often not the most important factor. Some individuals can drink relatively small quantities and still have a drinking problem. Others may put away more and not be alcoholic. The major issue is the *pattern* of alcohol consumption and also the effect on the drinker's ability to function with daily responsibilities and relationships.

You should ask these questions about yourself and also your partner:

- Have you ever lost control during drinking? That is, have you become violent or otherwise experienced a major behavior change?
- On a number of occasions, have you taken a drink just before you've driven an automobile?
- Have you ever been arrested for drunk driving?
- Have you ever had a blackout?
- Have you ever missed a day of work because of drinking or a hangover?
- Do you drink at lunch on weekdays?
- Do you drink three times or more a week?
- Have you ever been diagnosed as suffering from a liver problem or stomach bleeding?
- Have you ever gotten into physical fights since adolescence?
- Have you ever had the morning "shakes"?
- Has anyone suggested that you might be drinking too much?

Answering "yes" to even one question warrants professional consultation. An inexpensive and effective way to do this is to pay a visit to Alcoholics Anonymous, which has chapters throughout the United States. AA groups are self-run and make no charge for their services. Also, all chapters have frequent open meetings, where you're always welcome. But be forewarned: Since "it takes one to know one," you'll find you can't easily fool a recovering alcoholic about whether or not you have a problem.

If you think that you are an alcoholic or are in danger of becoming one, you must avoid marriage until you take effective steps to deal with the problem. Furthermore, by AA standards, marriage should be postponed until at least one year after the alcoholic has maintained a consistent state of sobriety.

Similarly, if the person you intend to marry shows signs of being an alcoholic, we urge frankness and restraint. Neither of you will benefit from a hasty leap into marriage. If he or she refuses to admit the problem, you've probably lost the game before you start. Alcoholics Anonymous or some other form of intensive counseling should be an absolute prerequisite before you make any kind of permanent commitment.

Finally, if you're already married to an alcoholic, you might take a cue from the experience of Francine and Dave. You're not going to help your marriage or your partner by denying or ignoring the problem.

So join a nondrinker's group like Al-Anon or ACOA (Adult Children of Alcoholics) and begin to develop techniques to confront your partner's drinking in a firm but loving way. If the marriage crumbles as a result of this pressure, so be it. Any other course of action will most likely condemn your spouse to personal failure and poor health, and your marriage to oblivion.

The Pain of Cocaine

Cocaine has replaced marijuana as the prestige drug of the current generation. This substance is by all criteria at least as dangerous as heroin. It may not be as addicting physically, but it is probably more habituating psychologically.

Crack and other potent forms of cocaine are particularly insidious. In fact, many experts feel there's no more dangerous drug than crack, which is so seductive that many individuals become hooked after using it only once or twice. The user feels euphoric after a few puffs, "speeded up" and sitting on top of the world. But the high is very short-lived, and unless more crack is readily available, the user rapidly comes crashing down.

The pattern of cocaine use is very different from that of heroin or other "street" drugs. Cocaine and its derivatives seem to permeate all levels of society, including the professional and well-to-do classes. Heroin is injected and is used mainly by men: cocaine is smoked or snorted and is equally popular with both sexes.

Cindy's Encounter with Cocaine

Cindy accepted Brad's social use of cocaine as just part of the fast crowd that he ran with as a stockbroker. He was making more than $200,000 annually, and money was no obstacle to his purchase of the drug. Also, he claimed that he didn't use it that much and could stop anytime he wanted to. The cocaine apparently had no negative impact on Brad's work performance or social abilities.

Despite some misgivings about his drug use, Cindy decided that she liked everything else about Brad, so she accepted when he proposed. Things went along rather well in the first six months of their marriage, though Cindy soon discovered that Brad was a much heavier cocaine user than he had led her to believe.

Then, a crisis struck. The stock market turned down, and Brad's earnings fell precipitously. He could no longer afford his cocaine habit, but he found he needed the drug even more as an escape from his business problems. As a result, he directed less and less money to their entertainment, their vacations and the upkeep of their country home, and more and more to his drug habit.

With the increased cocaine use, this couple's sex life went steadily downhill, a typical side effect of all types of drug abuse. When they finally came in for counseling, Brad was still holding down his job, but he had received several warnings from his employer about his poor performance and lack of punctuality.

Unfortunately, Brad was too deeply enmeshed in his cocaine habit to be able to recover without hospitalization. On the bright side, he was forced to make a choice because he was confronted by his employer with an ultimatum: Either he would take a leave of absence and seek some serious medical help, or he would be fired. As a result, he entered a rehabilitation program and is now on the road to recovery—as is his marriage with Cindy.

The Insidious Path of Drug Abuse

Drug addiction doesn't always start illicitly, as it did with Brad. Many people get hooked on medicines prescribed by doctors for pain, insomnia or weight control. After a while, though, these patients find they cannot live without the drugs. When the doctor cuts off the medications, they seek the same solace through illegal channels.

Pain is frequently treated with narcotics or opiates, agents very much like heroin. Besides analgesia, the effect of these drugs is to calm the individual and relax him. Pain medicines are also extremely physically addicting, and withdrawal is accompanied by a host of unpleasant physical symptoms. Sleeping pills or sedatives, though chemically somewhat different, cause very similar problems to narcotics.

In a similar vein, diet clinics are notorious for overprescribing amphetaminelike drugs. However, these agents are more effective in speeding up people than in causing any real weight loss. Patients get hooked on diet pills because they feel energized. Depression seems to melt away. In fact, the effects of amphetamines are very similar to those of cocaine.

Like alcoholism, drug abuse is characterized by a great deal of denial, as happened in the case of Brad and Cindy. The individual might admit to using drugs, particularly if he is caught red-handed, but he will insist that there isn't any problem. Also, he may accuse you of being uptight or closed-minded, and probably will insist that you get off his back.

If you force him to choose between you and his favorite drug, don't be surprised if you come in second best. It's much wiser and more effective to work hand in hand with a professional counselor, or even with an employer, as Cindy did.

Drug abuse can be cured, but only if the individual is willing to make a commitment to outside help. It's rare for the addict to be able to take care of the problem entirely by himself. Professional treatment or the support of a self-help group like Narcotics Anonymous is usually essential.

As for the Compatibility Quotient, there are few things that undermine marital peace and stability as profoundly as drug abuse. There's absolutely no future in marrying someone who is using drugs, particularly if that person is denying the problem and apparently has no interest in discontinuing the substance.

The Addict As Gambler

A problem closely related to substance abuse is pathological or compulsive gambling. Unfortunately, if our practice is any indication, this problem seems to be getting worse rather than better.

Not so many years ago, almost all gambling in this country was strictly illegal, with the activity at Las Vegas being one of the few exceptions. Now, casino gambling has spread, with the second major center now residing across the country in Atlantic City. Even more important, there has been a proliferation of government-sanctioned gambling, including official state lotteries. A variety of wagering like off-track betting is often condoned and may even be sponsored by state governments.

Of course, compulsive gambling existed long before the recent trends toward legal betting. Bookies, numbers runners and other stalwarts of illegal gambling catered to a substantial clientele throughout the early part of this century.

More recently, the number of individuals with gambling problems has increased in direct proportion to the burgeoning of opportunities. Even the casinos have now accepted some responsibility to provide funds to rehabilitate the addicts they help create.

Experts in pathological gambling liken the condition to excessive drinking. For most people, gambling, like drinking, is a harmless pleasure. Most individuals who partake have no trouble controlling their behavior. The average person may enjoy an informal wager every now and then, but most can take it or leave it.

A small number, though, are vulnerable to getting caught up in a vicious cycle: They start to play, then feel a slowly building tension, which has been described to us by some addicts as a form of intense but unconsummated sexual desire. If they lose, they feel compelled to continue and try to recoup their losses. If they win, the tension builds still further, and they are driven to play for higher and higher stakes.

Interestingly, the current treatment for compulsive gambling is patterned after Alcoholics Anonymous. As with alcoholism, Gamblers Anonymous sees the basic problem as a loss of control. The cure begins by acknowledging the illness and the addict's acceptance of the fact that he or she is powerless to control it.

Like recreational drinking, gambling is a pastime both partners can share. Perhaps you enjoy gambling and you are attracted to someone because the two of you share common interests. Beware, however, when the person you think you love seems more turned on by cards than by sex. Those who are preoccupied with gambling make very risky marriage partners—a fact that we have made clear in the Compatibility Quotient.

How can you identify a pathological gambler? In other words, how can you tell if your own gambling or that of your boyfriend or girlfriend has gotten out of hand?

To find out, put these questions to your partner, then ask them of yourself:

- Has he ever tried to stop gambling, but without success?
- Has she spent more money on gambling activities than she can easily afford?
- Is he preoccupied with gambling? For example, does he think about it during your dates or during work?
- Has she ever experienced periods of restlessness or irritability when there were no opportunities to gamble?
- Has he felt compelled to make up losses by increasing his level of betting?
- Has she found herself increasing the size of her bets in order to maintain a high level of excitement?

If you or your partner answers "yes" to any of these questions, there may be a problem. If there are two or more "yes" answers, the gambling has clearly reached pathological proportions and the person with the problem should avoid any marital commitments.

Up to this point, we've been focusing on how one problem personality can disturb the tranquility of a marriage. But there's another important set of potential difficulties that arises from the mix of two different people in one relationship. To respond to these issues, we've devoted the next part to what we've called the "mix of a marriage."

The Mix of a Marriage

Opposites Attract— But Do They Stay Together?

Sometimes, two different people may fall in love, and, against all predictions from their family and friends, they may go on to establish a durable relationship. No one would ever have thought that this crabby woman and that suspicious guy could make a go of it—yet they turn out to be the perfect couple!

More common, though, is the scenario of two attractive individuals, personable and well rounded in most respects. They find each other and get married, and it seems that they have everything going for them. But then, a few years later, the marriage falls apart. What forces and factors can cause such devastation?

Or take another well-known pattern: A man and woman live together harmoniously for two, three or five years. Perhaps they even have a child. Then one day, they decide to make it official and get married. Nothing has changed, supposedly, except for a legal piece of paper. But after the marriage ceremony, the two stop getting along, and six months later, they end up in divorce court. How can such a thing happen?

In this part of the book, we'll consider those issues that most often cause conflict as a result of the *mix* of the two personalities in a marriage. Among other things, we'll answer such questions as

- Are you better off marrying someone who is just like you, or should you look for your opposite?
- How are marriages affected by children, sex and money?
- What makes for good communication in a love relationship?
- What if my partner's parents are divorced?
- What if my partner is unemployed?
- What's the danger if we are of different religions?
- Is there a problem if my partner's been married before?

These and other "marriage mix" questions are now on the agenda—and the first issue we'll deal with is the truth about opposites.

The Truth about Opposites

It's firmly accepted in folklore that opposites attract. You know the stereotype: What can be more exciting for a conservative guy than the flamboyant redhead who is the life of the party? Or how great it can make a shy young woman feel to have the school's star athlete making a play for her!

In the long run, though, it's the similarity of a couple's values, not their differences, that bodes well for the durability of a marriage. Five years down the road, that attractive party doll might be seen by her husband as a spendthrift, a scatterbrain or an irresponsible child. Or the handsome, graceful star of the football team may turn out to be incapable of handling himself in the business world and making a decent living.

Couples tend to have a high CQ if they truly are compatible in temperament and personality traits. It just makes life easier.

If you're frugal, for instance, you'll appreciate your spouse if he is frugal too. If you love to skydive, you'll feel more at home with a partner who shares your lust for thrills. And if you are a physical fitness buff, chances are you'll have unending conflict and a loss of respect for a mate who sees little point in emphasizing good nutrition and exercise.

Complementarity is important, but this is a slightly different concept from similarity. You complement your wife if she is all thumbs and you are very handy. She complements your awkwardness with her social grace. At least one of you should be able to balance a checkbook. By bringing together different skills and aptitudes in these ways, you can accomplish more together than either of you could manage alone—*if* your respective skills and gifts *add* to the total relationship.

The important point is this: Your *values* must be the same, but not necessarily all your talents or your skills. Without similar values, your Compatibility Quotient will plummet; with different abilities and aptitudes, the CQ may go up.

Another important risk factor that relates to the opposites issue in many relationships is large differences in social or economic background. Marrying too far up or down the social scale is certainly a risk. It's also well known that marriages mixed in race or religion are under greater stress.

We're not suggesting that you marry a clone of yourself, of course. Even if you found one, he or she would probably bore you to death. Yet the success and satisfaction of a marriage often hinges on the shared enjoyment of the small things of life. Couples can have their differences, but they also need a large common ground. In general, husbands and wives who don't enjoy doing anything together have a low Compatibility Quotient.

How Does Your Personal Marriage Style Measure Up to Your Mate's?

To begin to get a handle on what it means to be the "opposite" of someone else in a love relationship, it's helpful to think in terms of marriage styles. Cliff Sager, a pioneer in marital therapy, has said that people starting out in a marriage can be divided into seven basic types:

- Some want true equality. They want to share and share alike.
- Some are purely rational; they relate entirely with their brains.
- Others are complete romantics. To them, marriage is a matter of the heart.
- Some individuals enter into marriage wanting to be a parent.
- Others want to play the role of a child.
- Still others seek a lifetime companion, and passion isn't an overriding consideration.
- Finally, there are people who want little more than a reliable roommate to share their bills.

Any of these seven types can help make a good marriage, but ultimate success depends on the mix between the two people, and how the combination stands up over time.

For example, a woman who is by nature a take-charge type will often be attracted to a man who likes to follow and have others make decisions for him. This kind of mix can last for many years, or even permanently. But what if the husband decides he wants to grow up? Or suppose the wife gets sick and tired of playing the leader role?

These roles, by the way, are not limited or determined by gender. For example, the person who is the "parent" in a parent-child type of marriage may be the woman as well as the man.

One such female "parent" was Jackie, a thirty-four-year-old investment banker, who called us for an emergency session after her husband, Ralph, walked out. We had followed this couple for several years, ostensibly to help Ralph deal with his many problems. Jackie was seemingly the "well one" in the marriage, stable and capable and never needing outside help. When we all met together, we always seemed to end up with three therapists—Jackie and the two of us! There was only one patient—poor ol' Ralph.

It seemed that Ralph could never do anything right. He had attended an impressive college and had studied anthropology with several professors famous in their fields. He finished his formal courses years ago and did some research on his dissertation from time to time. But in general, he still regarded himself as a student, intellectual and writer.

For a long time, Ralph didn't go out to look for regular work. Instead, he stayed at home writing, or at least thinking about writing. Jackie worked long days and on weekends too, not just to earn money but also to make a mark in her high-powered Wall Street job. For a long time, she didn't worry that Ralph had turned into a perpetual student. After all, she earned enough for both of them.

This couple's major problems began when their child was born. For his part, Ralph was thrilled with his new son, and he easily incorporated him into his stay-at-home routine. But somehow, Jackie was expected to help with exactly 50 percent of the child care tasks, and not always the most pleasant ones. For example, Ralph made her responsible for all the pediatrician's visits because he had trouble with the sight of blood, needles and other medical things.

They decided to move to a larger apartment in an exclusive neighborhood, and for the first time, they experienced some financial pressure. As a result, Ralph agreed to get a "real" job as a substitute teacher at the local high school. Though the pay wasn't the best, Jackie was glad that her husband had finally gotten out of the house. At the same time, though, she felt guilty that his job was interfering with his studies and the completion of his doctoral dissertation.

Only a few months after starting work, Ralph became depressed and had to take a leave of absence. He beat his breast with guilt for letting Jackie down, but this only aggravated his depressed state. Although he attempted to return to work as a teacher on a number of occasions, each time he had a relapse into depression. At home he wept a lot, sometimes in the presence of his young son.

To no one's surprise, the couple started having marriage problems. Most spouses who come for marital therapy scream and bicker with each other, but not this one. Jackie told us of frustration after frustration, and Ralph just hung his head and wept.

We pointed out to Jackie that she must stop trying to be Ralph's "good mommy," because it wasn't helping. So she pulled back and let him do things on his own. Still, each time there was a crisis, Jackie couldn't constrain herself from taking charge.

Finally, in an unusual show of independence, Ralph decided to leave home to see if he could work his life out better on his own. "I don't regard this as a permanent thing," he said. "But I feel I just have to find my way apart from Jackie's influence."

Interestingly, Ralph has fared better than his wife since the separation. He rented an apartment in the same building so that he could be near his son. Also, he remained on very friendly terms with Jackie. But he now firmly declines all her offers of financial help or advice about his life.

Another positive sign is that Ralph works regularly now because he *has* to; he knows Jackie can't support two separate households. Also, Ralph is making more progress on his dissertation. In addition, he's cooking, cleaning and exercising, and in general beginning to feel great about himself.

As for Jackie, she seems to be in mourning, like an overprotective mother whose beloved only child has gone away to college. Always the chronic rescuer, she now has no one left to pull out of the burning building. More importantly, she's having to learn to relinquish her role as surrogate parent with her husband and to treat him on a more equal basis.

Ironically, although this couple continues to be separated, they seem to be developing a healthier relationship with one another. We hope that Jackie and Ralph will eventually reconcile, because they are quite compatible in many ways. On the other hand, a long-term separation could work against their marriage because each will continue to move in more independent directions, and the inevitable result will be that they'll drift apart. If they do get back together, however, it must be on a more adult-to-adult basis.

Opposites May Not Remain Opposites

One of the most important principles that we want to get across in this book is that over time, partners change, and as a result, marriages change. Furthermore, this principle applies to opposites as well as to those who start out a relationship with quite similar interests and orientations.

Take, for example, the autocratic husband and the passive, somewhat helpless wife. She has always been more than glad to let him run the show. But what if he gets sick? Or suppose he's fired from his job, or he's overwhelmed with business problems— what happens then?

Even the most dependent spouse must be prepared to take charge, at least temporarily, in times of real crisis. When the danger is past, the pair's relationship can revert to its original state. But a childlike spouse with absolutely no ability to cope will wear the patience of even the most accomplished and self-reliant despot.

The "mix" of a marriage, then, is not a static combination. It must be flexible enough to meet the demands of life as they present themselves over the years. As a general rule, the CQ is quite low for rigid, inelastic partners, even if they seem to be compatible at first.

Does Your Partner Clash or Complement?

The basic principle we're formulating here involves a balance between complementarity and clashing. That is, you should try to find somebody who complements your weaknesses and inadequacies, but at the same time doesn't clash too much with your basic needs and personality type.

To know whether you and your partner will clash or comple-ment, a necessary first step is to be realistic and honest in your evaluations of one another, and then of the two of you together. As you proceed with this evaluation, you should recognize at the outset that there's no one style of marriage or combination of part-ners that is absolutely right.

In fact, you may be able to establish a happy, long-term rela-tionship with *several* different types of partners. A big mistake, though, is to pretend to be something other than what you really are, or to pretend that your partner is something other than what he or she really is.

For example, an overbearing man raised in an old-fashioned, domineering family will probably delude himself if he asserts that he wants a marriage based on equal sharing of power. Of course, he may genuinely decide to reject his background and past atti-tudes and begin to experience a real change. But that's different from self-deception, which can seriously undercut the compatibil-ity potential of a relationship.

How Mort Fooled Himself

Mort was a guy who fell prey to this sort of self-deception. He was rigid, isolated and rather cold in his relationships with others. In these characteristics, he was almost a carbon copy of his father. But because of an intense adolescent rebellion against his father's authority, he had convinced himself that the two of them were quite different—and that was the beginning of his problems.

Having been something of a student radical, Mort had given outward support to the early women's liberation movement. Even though he worked earnestly for the feminist program, however, he was really motivated not by any genuine commitment to wom-en's rights, but rather by a desire to get back at the "establish-ment"—which undoubtedly reminded him of his father.

At heart, Mort was also something of a misanthrope. To twist the Will Rogers saying, he never met a person, man or woman, that he didn't dislike in some way. But to his credit, he did feel ashamed of his natural instincts to control and boss women.

Mort married Abby, who was a sweet, nice person but who tended to be unsure of herself. He bullied her into taking radical feminist stands and ordered her to divide the tasks of their marriage along strictly equal lines. In the process, Mort berated her when she was not sufficiently egalitarian to satisfy him, and he didn't hesitate to browbeat her.

The few friends the couple had knew that Mort was a phony. But Abby didn't see through his facade, at least not at first. Gradually, however, over a period of several years, Abby matured and developed a stronger personality. After their two children were born, she quickly saw that Mort wasn't really interested in true equality because now, sharing the household and child-rearing responsibilities threatened to cut into his free time for reading and political action meetings.

Abby was stuck both with the full child care duties and with increasing cleaning and cooking around the home. Furthermore, Mort started pushing her to increase her outside employment from a part-time to a full-time job: "With the kids' expenses, we just can't make ends meet unless you contribute more," Mort said.

Finally, the burdens became too much and she balked. The first signs of resistance came in the form of anger, which she unloaded on Mort for what seemed to him to be innocuous comments, such as, "Didn't you get any orange juice today?" Or, "This apartment is really a mess, and I have a committee that's coming over here tonight."

The couple began to get into loud shouting matches, and finally they sought counseling. Although it was hard for Mort to back up and understand what he had been doing, he finally realized that his expectations for his marriage had been wrong. The event that triggered his turnaround was his wife's threat to get a divorce. He became genuinely afraid of losing his family. He had wanted equality and a radical lifestyle, but now adjustments had to be made to the realities of his domestic situation if he wanted the marriage to survive.

Among other things, he needed to place fewer demands on Abby and also to take over more of the household and child care duties. That meant cutting back on some of his outside activities. Deciding what to retain and what to eliminate was particularly difficult. But like a number of others we have counseled, Mort finally realized—quite literally at the last minute of his marriage—how much he had to lose. Many fathers, as well as mothers, become intensely motivated to make their marriage work when it finally dawns on them that they may be separated from their children and from the relatively stable home life they have enjoyed.

These opposites were able to make a midcourse change in their marriage and now seem well on the way to a more successful union. Compromise, accepting differences and learning how to negotiate are the keys to complementarity—and to helping opposites stay together.

Of course, individuals often function in unpredictable ways when they get involved in new relationships. They may feel and do things they never thought were possible when they were alone, such as traveling, returning to college or learning new skills. Also, people often change in positive directions or suddenly mature emotionally after major life events, such as having children. So, if you're currently married to an opposite and the combination seems headed toward trouble, there is still hope.

The challenge is to be honest and realistic in evaluating yourself and your partner. This sort of evaluation, accompanied by a courtship of a year if you're not yet married, should tell you better whether you can get along permanently with this person, or whether you should look elsewhere.

THIRTEEN

The Family Mix

The families we come from, the experiences we've undergone growing up, the contacts we've had with brothers and sisters, the philosophy we've developed about having our own children—all these have a powerful effect on the Compatibility Quotient.

One simple exercise is to spend some time at family gatherings observing how our partner's mother and father relate to one another, and also how they relate to their children. In this way, you can gain important clues about the future of your current relationship. A man who is unable to give up his mother's cooking, or a woman who seems to have an ongoing crush on her "daddy" may have a hard time establishing a workable marital bond.

Claire came to see us when she began to date Harold. She liked many things about him, but she was always disquieted by what seemed to be an unhealthy closeness he had to his family, especially his mother. She was optimistic, however, that marriage would help him break away.

Then, things began to go seriously wrong much sooner than she had expected. She asked for an appointment to see us barely a week after the wedding, and almost as soon as she walked through the door, she began to complain bitterly about the way the marriage had begun.

"Some honeymoon!" she said in exasperation. "We went to Niagara Falls and took the bridal suite we had booked a year in advance. Everything was sexy and exciting, and I thought we'd spend the entire week in bed.

"The wedding night was fine. There were no surprises, but we had always gotten along well sexually. The next morning, though, Harold just moped around, and he became more and more glum as the week wore on.

"When I finally asked him what was wrong, he confessed to me that he missed his mother. 'Confessed' is somewhat inaccurate— he actually bragged about it, as though being lonely for your mother is some kind of virtue. He missed her food, her company, her fussing over him.

"There was no use fighting it. We came home three days early and headed straight for Mama's house. After a big meal of her lasagne and stewed apples, Harold was fine again, and as sexy as ever with me."

Those too dependent on their parents can make questionable spouses, though many of them eventually do grow up. Their CQ remains low, however, as long as the new couple stays overly dependent on the extended family, either financially, physically or emotionally.

The flip side of this phenomenon also presents problems: Men and women who have had very unhappy childhoods tend to get involved in unstable marriages, for all their good intentions to avoid the mistakes of their parents. Children from strife-filled homes often have high rates of divorce, whether their parents have remained together or separated.

According to classic studies by Lewis Terman and then by Ernest Burgess and Leonard Cottrell, two of the most significant predictors of marital success are the marital happiness of each spouse's parents and the contentment of each spouse's own childhood. If our experience with thousands of patients is any indication, these findings are as true as ever.

Still, it's important to approach this issue with some degree of balance: Preparing for marriage may require a certain degree of independence, but it doesn't require a complete emotional or physical estrangement from your folks.

In fact, the CQ is low for people who are extremely resentful about their experiences in growing up, or who have completely cut themselves off from their families of origin. If no one shows up for your wedding, you ought to take a hint that you may be heading for trouble!

As we've indicated elsewhere, the CQ is also low whenever there is a great disparity between the economic, social, racial or religious backgrounds of the partners. Marrying from a poor into a rich family, or from an educated into an uneducated one, always boosts the chances for divorce. Of course, we're not advocating that those from broken homes or other problems in their family history or cultural background avoid marriage! Rather, if you do have any of these risk factors, you should discuss them with your prospective spouse and perhaps seek counseling.

Does It Help to Have Brothers and Sisters?

Psychologist Walter Toman has carried out landmark studies to answer this question: Is there a strong connection between the structure of the family of origin and the ultimate success of a marriage? His classic work *Family Constellation* contains some rather startling conclusions.

First of all, having brothers and sisters seems to prepare an individual well for marriage. According to Toman, only children who marry only children have a divorce rate as much as five times as great as those who have siblings.

One explanation for this phenomenon is that youngsters without brothers or sisters don't learn to share as well as those with siblings. As a result, they end up being unprepared for the give-and-take of married life.

Having siblings seems to help you prepare for marriage, and having siblings of the opposite sex is even better. The explanation for the gender factor is fairly straightforward: Boys who grow up only with other brothers tend to view the female sex as somewhat mysterious. Boys with sisters, on the other hand, are quite familiar with the ways of girls. Similarly, girls who have grown up with brothers learn from an early age—and often with a great deal of sympathetic understanding—what boys have to go through in establishing their male identity and handling acceptance and rejection by their peers.

Another relevant factor that Toman identified was what he called age rank. For example, he found that oldest brothers should be wary of marrying oldest sisters, and vice versa. The reason: Firstborns tend to be bossy and highly competitive, while younger siblings are often much more easygoing. A marriage between firstborns is a setup for a constant power struggle.

As with our discussion of opposites in the previous chapter, a controlling principle here is complementarity. In other words, your experience in the birth order in your own family should complement that of your partner—but it's best for those experiences not to be the same.

Practically speaking, if you are the oldest child in your family, try to find a spouse who is a younger child in his. Conversely, if you are the youngest, look for someone with experience in being an older sibling.

Toman's basic rule for staying out of trouble with this sibling-order issue is what he calls the "duplication theorem." This rule states that in your marriage you ought to try to duplicate the structure of your original family.

An ideal arrangement, for example, would be for an oldest girl, who has one or two younger brothers, to marry a youngest boy, who has one or two older sisters. In this situation, each partner has grown up with a peer of the opposite sex, and the spouses complement each other in their age ranks. The girl is used to younger siblings, and the boy is used to older ones.

How Neil and Barbara Benefited from Their Birth Order

By most standards, Neil and Barbara were a most unlikely couple. Yet their marriage appears to be thriving, in large part because of their family backgrounds.

Barbara is the firstborn child of a large immigrant family. Her parents were warm, outgoing people with a wide circle of friends. Understandably, her fondest childhood memories are of mealtimes, where there was always a lot of noise and fun. During the many courses, everyone's personal problems were fair game for discussion.

Barbara grew into a lively young woman who would look you in the eye and tell you exactly what was on her mind. She did well in college and law school and had just begun her first job as corporation counsel when she met Neil.

Neil's background was quite different. He grew up in a small town on the West Coast, where his family's roots went back for many generations. The men were master carpenters as long ago as the Gold Rush, and Neil never considered doing anything else for a living.

Neil's parents were quiet people who showed their love in deeds, not words. Dinner was usually served in pleasant silence, and privacy was a major virtue. One quickly learned not to interfere or use too many words with other people. Whereas Barbara was gregarious and voluble, Neil was gentle and patient, even phlegmatic to the point of being very quiet much of the time.

Despite these differences, these two people have made a solid, happy marriage. Curious, we asked Neil for his secret.

"I really don't know," he told us amiably.

Then Barbara interjected, "Look, despite the big difference in our backgrounds, being married to Neil feels very comfortable. I was the oldest child in my family. I had many responsibilities at home, looking after my two younger sisters and my little brother. But I was also given a great deal of power.

"Neil was a change-of-life baby. His parents had three girls, and they were about to call it quits on having any more. But then his mom got pregnant, and when Neil was born, the whole family went nuts. His father now had the boy he had always wanted, a son who could work with him in his trade. Neil's mother and his older sisters doted on him, happily looking after him and telling him what to do."

We thought we got the point, but we asked Barbara to be more specific.

"You see," Barbara continued, "Neil and I have always fit together very smoothly. I'm a take-charge person, like his sisters. He's much more laid back, like my younger brother. We both feel very much at home."

"Right," said Neil. "I agree."

Obviously, even though they were so different in many ways, the experiences of these two people in their respective families, including their places in the birth order, had worked to their decided advantage.

How Your Own Children Can Affect Compatibility

It has been said with some accuracy that the only issues married people ever fight about are money, sex and children. Spouses are rarely in total agreement about the size and spacing of their family or the way they want to raise their kids, so parenting styles are often a major source of disagreement.

One spouse may be permissive and trusting, while the other believes in firm control. Not only will the children get confusing messages in this atmosphere, but also the disparate styles can lead to endless conflict.

On the other hand, there is no doubt that the presence of children is a major deterrent to divorce. Despite the fact that one-parent families have now gained a considerable degree of social respectability, many people still stay together largely for the children. When they finally split, they do so after the children leave home.

Of course, there is a downside to having children under the wrong circumstances. In particular, having a child too soon will lower the Compatibility Quotient, not raise it. Many studies have shown that premarital pregnancy, even having children within the first year of marriage, will greatly increase the probability of eventual divorce. A major problem is the economic pressure on a young couple burdened too soon with a child. Certainly, the premature arrival of a baby disrupts the courtship process and the early break-in period of a marriage. In general, then, having a child too soon will cut short the necessary stage of preparation for a stable marriage.

Our advice is to consider having children only when you are reasonably certain the relationship is working. Giving birth too early will undermine the marriage, not strengthen it. You'll most likely find that you just haven't had sufficient time to work out the differences in your relationship. A baby can be the catalyst to cause those differences to explode.

On the other hand, you may find you have no choice. In that case, you must work extra hard to keep your marriage healthy by concentrating on the two of you, not just on your baby. For example, it's essential to earmark special times to get to know one another, without the constant distraction of a howling infant. A number of couples have discovered that going out on a regular weekly "date" serves this purpose quite well.

Under no circumstances should you assume that just because you have a child, your marriage will go on automatically or your spouse won't leave you. Instead, you must continue to act like lovers with each other, and your role as parents will be strengthened as a result.

FOURTEEN

The Sex Factor

Sex, many feel, is the great barometer of marital success. People who are sexually compatible, the argument goes, should have some sort of guarantee of an enduring marriage.

Unfortunately, it just doesn't work this way.

Although it may seem like ancient history, it really wasn't so long ago that most men and women didn't sleep together before marriage. Many young people were virgins, and proud of it. From necking and petting, the couple might have made some educated guesses about the way they would hit it off sexually, but the first true taste of sexual compatibility typically took place on the wedding night. Furthermore, despite the lack of premarital sampling, most marriages in the old days stayed together.

Premarital intercourse is now quite commonplace, of course, and many don't lift an eyebrow when two young people live together. Some still assume that more experience will give modern couples a better shot at lasting sexual compatibility than their forebears. Yet there is no good evidence that couples today are any more harmonious in bed than those in the past. In fact, according to a 1989 study of government data by researchers from the University of Wisconsin, which we've cited in an earlier chapter, those who live together before marriage get divorced at a higher rate than those who don't live together.

In this same vein, back in 1938 Lewis Terman, a Stanford University psychologist, attempted to debunk the myth that good sex is the key to happy marriage. His research at that time found little or no correlation between sexual intercourse and marital contentment—at least in terms of frequency of sex acts. Terman's findings have been confirmed repeatedly over the last fifty years. In her book *Is There Sex After Marriage?*, Carol Botwin exhaustively documents the scarcity of sexual contact in many stable modern marriages.

Now, don't get us wrong! We don't want to convey the impression that sex means nothing in marriage. Rather, the main point is that good sex isn't a consistent predictor of marital success. Certainly, it's not as important a factor as the couple's style of communication or economic situation. Young lovers may enjoy each other sexually and still fight about everything else. In fact, constantly feuding couples may be quite passionate under the sheets; even divorced husbands and wives have been known to continue highly satisfying sex lives.

On the other hand, there are a number of situations in which bad sex of various types can inject a negative and disruptive Sex Factor into a relationship.

When Sex Can Make a Big Difference

The Sex Factor comes into play in a couple's overall compatibility with at least eight different types of partners: mismatched partners, the undersexed partner, the oversexed partner, the power-through-sex partner, the garden-variety cheater, the womanizer, the homosexual, and the sexual deviant.

MISMATCHED PARTNERS.

Marital stability is further threatened by markedly different attitudes about sexual values or sexual practices. For example, there is likely to be trouble if one partner is genuinely straitlaced and the other gets turned on by kinkiness.

Sexual compatibility is most important at the extremes of desire and performance. Here, on the edges of normality, the risks of divorce can be enormous. Gross incompatibility in what the man and the woman want will greatly decrease the CQ.

THE UNDERSEXED PARTNER.

Most predictive of divorce is a consistent lack of sexual desire in one of the partners, even before marriage. But note: The couple in which neither mate particularly likes sex may do all right.

Performance difficulties, such as premature ejaculation, situational impotence or an occasional or even frequent inability to have an orgasm, are not as serious. The main problem lies with those who are never "turned on" at all.

Total lack of heterosexual desire sometimes masks another issue, such as latent homosexuality or significant mental illness. Asexuality can be a satisfying and productive way of life, but there are better choices than marriage for individuals with no or little sexual desire. Wherever there is a total lack of interest, don't get insulted. Just get out! The problem is your partner's, not yours.

Wendy came to this conclusion after two years of on-again, off-again marriage plans with Rick.

"I always loved him, and I still love him," she said. "I think he loves me too, but not in a sexual way.

"I've done everything I could to entice him. Skimpy bathing suits, low-cut dresses, perfume, garter belts, everything, and hardly a rise—no pun intended.

"He has no religious or moral reservations about sex—I could understand that. It's just that he seems uninterested in sex under any circumstances, including kissing and caressing. He'd just rather do other things.

"I don't know much about Rick's past sexual background, and

I don't think I really want to know. If it turns out that he gets turned on by other women, that would make me feel awful. If he likes men, I'll feel like a fool. And if he's hopelessly sexless, well, that would be the worst news of all."

Wendy told us that she has vacillated between trying to rape Rick and leaving him alone. Yet neither strategy has produced results. Not only has there been no sexual intercourse, but Rick's lack of passion hasn't even moved them close to the bedroom.

Still, Wendy doesn't want to give him up. She thinks she'll change him yet. But if this couple marries—and Rick says he wants to—we predict that Wendy's unmet sexual needs will drive her to affairs, unending recriminations and, eventually, divorce.

THE OVERSEXED PARTNER.

Sometimes problems spring from too much desire. Terri and Josh saw us after they had been married eight years, and both agreed that their sexual pattern was the same as it had been from the first time they met. Josh loved sex. In particular, he loved having sex with Terri, and he readily admitted that she responded in a frequent and sensual manner. But that wasn't enough for him.

"I'm afraid of growing old," this thirty-five-year-old lawyer told us. "I don't know how much longer I'll have it, so I want to use it while I can. I'd like to do it every day, twice a day, three times. From the chandeliers, in the swimming pool, I don't care.

"I used to be an inhibited kid," he continued, "but ever since college, I've been very proud of my sexual prowess and my lack of inhibitions."

It soon became apparent that Josh was quite committed to his wife. He didn't want to leave her. In fact, he didn't even want to cheat on her. He simply wanted her to join him in his lusty activities.

Terri was no prude. She wasn't morally repelled by her husband's strong sexual tastes. In fact, she had agreed to rent X-rated videos and watch them with him while they tried new positions and styles of lovemaking.

"I like sex with Josh, even three or four times a week, which is more than most of my friends do it," she said. "But three times a day? No way. It isn't me. I like to go out and do other things sometimes."

Terri became resentful of Josh's constant innuendos that she was undersexed. She knew that wasn't true, but the thought was still chilling to her. She simply didn't share her husband's boundless sexual energy and his varied hungers. She finally decided that she no longer cared to keep up with him.

Just as the Compatibility Quotient was low for Wendy and Rick, it's also low for Terri and Josh. The men in these relationships are well off the scale of normal sexual desire, a condition that threatens the permanency of any marriage.

The best thing an undersexed person like Rick can do—provided he's not homosexual—is to find another partner who likes sex as little as he does. The outlook for an oversexed partner like Josh may be better, depending on the real reason for his excessive sexual desire and interest. If he has become compulsive about sex— that is, he desperately needs it, even though he doesn't particularly enjoy it—he's likely to lack sensitivity in his intimate relationship. But in fact, with Josh this isn't the case.

As he indicated to us, part of his problem is that he is rebelling against a restricted family background, and in some ways, he's still living out an adolescent fantasy. The only difference between his fantasies and that of most teenagers is that he wants to satisfy his flights of imagination within the confines of his marriage.

On the whole, then, Josh's attitudes and responses suggested a certain degree of compulsion or addiction, but he appeared to be willing to change. The first step was for him to understand how he was using sex as a substitute for intimacy. The next step was for him to reach some sort of compromise between his need for large doses of sex and Terri's understandable desire to broaden the range of her social life.

We suggested that Josh might enjoy sex even more if he would combine it with romantic dinners, dancing, movies and other cultural opportunities. "Accept these social events as part of the wooing process, part of the foreplay, and see what happens," we said.

Fortunately, Josh was concerned enough about the future of his marriage to go along with this idea. As for Terri, she found she became even more interested in sex after they came home from one of these outings because of the romantic atmosphere that had been created.

This couple is still working out an adjustment to their disparate needs, and so far they are succeeding. But for this approach to work, the oversexed person must be willing, as Josh was, to accommodate to the needs of the more normal partner in the relationship.

THE POWER-THROUGH-SEX PARTNER.

Sex connotes much more than intimacy or physical pleasure. The sex life of a couple mirrors many issues between them, from aesthetic sensibilities to struggles over power.

Sex can be used to curry favor, show displeasure or bludgeon the other person into submission. Many modern couples attempt to share responsibilities in the home or the workplace. When it comes to sex, however, reciprocity is harder to achieve. Sociologists Philip Blumstein and Pepper Schwartz, in their well-known study *American Couples*, state, "Initiation is still likely to be the husband's responsibility and refusal, the wife's prerogative."

When a man initiates and the woman refuses, he can always rationalize that she is "not in the mood." But when a woman initiates and the man refuses, she tends to take it personally and see it as a direct rejection of her.

On the whole, most American men initiate sexual intercourse more frequently than women. Perhaps complete reciprocity in both sexual initiation and refusal is consistent with a very satisfying sex life. But that equal give-and-take just doesn't reflect reality. In most cases, men must expect to be the ones who take the lead in the bedroom.

On the other hand, sexual role reversal, with the woman taking charge most of the time, seems to make many couples unhappy. Although some have objected that this observation smacks of sexism, it nonetheless reflects the facts about many relationships.

Furthermore, men often seem to feel threatened when their partners consistently want sex more often than they do. In the end, the woman who is too sexually aggressive may provoke a backlash of insecurity and inadequacy in her partner, and both sexual frequency and satisfaction may suffer. As a general rule, the CQ goes down when the woman is always the sexual pursuer and the man is always holding back.

THE GARDEN-VARIETY CHEATER.

While every marriage is at risk for extramarital affairs, some combinations of partners are at higher risk than others. In his excellent book *More Than Just a Friend*, Tom McGinnis has analyzed the characteristics of people who are more likely to cheat on their mates, and those who are less likely. We see a parallel with the Compatibility Quotient because the same underlying personality characteristics that lead people to have affairs also tend to lead to divorce. The CQ questionnaire has been designed with these traits in mind.

For example, individuals who are adventurous, rebellious or self-willed are more likely to fool around during the marriage. They may also be at higher risk to leave it when the marriage no longer suits them.

Furthermore, people who fear intimacy and emotional involvement seem to lack the commitment either to stay faithful or to remain married. Impulsive individuals are also high risks for both cheating and divorce.

On the other hand, conformists and people who live by strict ethical principles tend to avoid affairs and stay married, though there are exceptions. Others who are likely to be faithful are those who are devoutly religious, those who are timid or childlike, and those who are worried about "what the neighbors will think."

For a marriage to make it without a disruptive affair, however, the traditional, faithful person must not be engaged in activities or habits that either directly or indirectly provoke the other partner. For example, workaholics or individuals who like rigid routines tend not to cheat, but their spouses do because they are often alone or bored. Ultimately, these marriages are at risk because the habits of one partner inherently alienate the other.

The risk is also high for couples who choose unusual lifestyles, such as "open" marriages, even if the choice is mutually and fairly arrived at. When one or both partners are constantly engaging in open, outside sexual activity, the marriage will most likely not survive very long.

The most malignant affairs, by the way, are those that occur during the courtship period, when commitment between the partners is supposed to be at an all-time high. The man or woman who cheats on his or her intended in the week before the wedding probably won't stay married long.

THE WOMANIZER.

Womanizing by definition is almost exclusively a male phenomenon, though we would allow for the possibility of what might be called "manizing" among certain highly insecure, disturbed women.

Unlike the occasional cheater, the womanizer engages in a constant round of multiple affairs for the thrill of conquest. The more, the better for him, and most of his waking hours are spent planning new seductions or reliving old ones.

No woman, no matter how attractive or sexually satisfying, can hold this guy's exclusive attention for very long. Like Don Juan, the womanizer feels alive only when he is able to add an extra sexual "notch" to his record of conquests.

With few exceptions, this man's affairs produce deeply ingrained habits during his single years and usually carry over after the wedding day to destabilize the marriage. The CQ will go down dramatically, with a great increase in risk for divorce, when the man's emotional entanglements occur frequently, are characterized by a need for conquest, and are accompanied by reckless behavior.

One man we counseled actually seemed to have a death wish for his marriage because he would frequently flirt with other women in his wife's presence, then ask them out on dates where he might be seen by the couple's friends. Needless to say, this marriage didn't last long.

Men who are true womanizers are extremely high divorce risks unless they marry wives who close their eyes tightly and ask no questions. But this solution doesn't make for a happy relationship, even if the marriage manages to hold together.

In general, then, womanizers make terrible marriage partners. They are in love with the chase, not the object, which is a woman with whom to build a permanent, stable family life. No one woman will do for these men, and those women who try to tame them in marriage are doomed to failure. In the end, the womanizer is in love with no one but himself.

THE HOMOSEXUAL.

A strong commitment to homosexuality has rarely been altered by marriage and frequently leads to divorce. It's true that some bisexuals or others with relatively mild homosexual inclinations have succeeded in establishing long-term, satisfying marriages with those of the opposite sex. But those with a long, mostly exclusive history of homosexual relationships are poor risks for marriage.

THE SEXUAL DEVIANT.

Finally, if a man has served time for rape or if he has a history of molesting children, his Compatibility Quotient is close to zero. It's well established that such people are unlikely to change and therefore have nothing to offer a partner looking for a stable marriage.

The Sex Factor, then, has a number of complex and sometimes confusing dimensions. In general, though, the problems and solutions in this area are often much simpler than they first appear: As a rule, we would recommend that you become concerned about the sexual issue only if your relationship is characterized by one or more of the above eight circumstances. Other less-than-perfect sexual situations usually can be resolved quite successfully with a little patience and a great deal of love and understanding.

FIFTEEN

The Matter of Money

Maggie and Bob were typical of the 1950s and 1960s. The two had met in college, and both grew up with the assumptions that they would have considerably more cash to operate on than either of their parents, that the husband should be the chief breadwinner, and that the wife should stay home and care for the kids.

They also came from similar cultural backgrounds, attended the same church and had families of similar economic means. In Maggie's mind, her major goal was to get married before graduation, and Bob, a Big Man On Campus, was certainly the most promising candidate around.

Marriage was a must in the view of most young women of that time. To graduate as a spinster at the ripe old age of twenty-one was a profound source of anxiety, not to mention humiliation.

Bob liked the idea of marriage too, though he wasn't quite as keen on it as Maggie. A good athlete, he was popular with most of his classmates, and he wondered if he might not find an even more suitable mate if he looked around a little more. He hesitated to give up his freedom by making a firm commitment too soon. Also, he wondered if maybe he was rushing into things; they had been dating seriously for only a couple of months.

But the idea of settling the marriage question sooner than later finally began to win him over. Besides, Maggie was attractive and popular too, a cheerleader who had never lacked for dates and would undoubtedly be scooped up by someone else if he didn't act without too much delay.

The decision became final when Maggie found she was pregnant at the end of her sophomore year. She automatically dropped out of school and set up housekeeping with two new sets of dishes and a stack of monogrammed sheets and towels. The thought of making a new home and cuddling a baby overcame any regrets about further education. After all, as they quipped in those days, she had gone to school to get her "Mrs." degree.

Bob went ahead and finished his college education, but he was too distracted as a new husband and father to perform up to his potential in his classes. As a result, he graduated with a less than stellar academic record.

Upon graduation, he took a minor supervisory job at the local power company, yet he was quite satisfied with his office responsibilities. His paycheck wasn't enormous by any means, but he felt he had at least started out on a promising career.

The first few years were kind enough to this couple. There was sufficient money to live reasonably well, and they were able to set aside some extra time to spend together as a family. Then, a second child came along, and a third, and Maggie found she was increasingly tied down to the home.

Now, the once-attractive college cheerleader became a bit plump and dowdy, an occupational hazard of raising children on limited funds and little help. Consequently, Maggie lapsed increasingly into despair.

Bob was in better shape at this point, both emotionally and physically. He was enjoying a limited sort of prosperity: After doling out Maggie's household allowance, he had enough pocket money to dress well and enough time to keep his athletic body trim and fit.

There were a number of fringe benefits, as well. The young women at his office found him quite attractive, and he succumbed to temptation periodically, with his wife none the wiser. As time went on, though, he took fewer and fewer pains to conceal his philandering activities from his wife. He felt an ever-dwindling sexual attraction for Maggie and rarely approached her in bed.

As for Maggie, she suffered in silence. Her own father had been the unquestioned master of his home, and she had been raised to think that being a lady meant not making a fuss. She was chronically fatigued and depressed, however, and moped around the house constantly, becoming less attractive to Bob than ever.

When their kids entered school, Maggie asked Bob's permission to take a job. She had good typing and steno skills, and a position had become available as secretary to the principal of the very school that the children attended. Bob assented hesitantly, mainly because the growing family constantly needed more money. He did feel a twinge of uneasiness, however, because what she was suggesting went beyond the realm of his family experience: His mother had never worked, and his father had always boasted, "I can earn enough without any woman's help!"

In any event, Maggie went to work, and the job made an enormous difference in her life. She began to lose weight and dress well. Her boss encouraged her to complete her college degree, and the school system picked up the costs of her tuition.

At home, her income became extremely important because Bob seriously injured his back and was forced to go on disability for several months. During this period, Maggie and the school principal started to spend more time together, and he provided a willing and sympathetic ear for her troubles at home. Among other things, she told him how Bob refused to do any housework or help at all with the kids, so that she ended up doing all that in addition to holding down a full-time job.

The principal, Mike, who was a somewhat older man, was divorced and lived alone. He was Maggie's biggest booster, and the two were soon spending many hours together, sharing common interests at work and becoming physically involved in his apartment.

Maggie especially resented Bob's lack of industry, and she steadily grew more contemptuous of him for failing to make a living. He made endless excuses about his back, but he also felt ashamed and worthless for relinquishing the role of breadwinner. Eventually, he did return to work, but at a limited-duty job that provided a salary about equal to that of his wife.

Finally, Bob came home one day to find his dinner prepared and a small note taped to the oven: "I am leaving you to live with Mike. I've taken the kids to my mother. I do not hate you. Perhaps someday we can be friends."

Why This Marriage Failed

Many risk factors are apparent in this marriage: the youth of the partners, their brief courtship, the surprise pregnancy, and a difference in communication styles. But the precipitating event for the split was economic.

When Bob began his career, he was able to call the shots, and his wishes generally prevailed. Maggie was so overwhelmed with housework and child care that she was unable to do more than get through each day. The balance of power was all in Bob's favor.

The day that Maggie returned to work, however, the balance of power began to shift. The unwritten rules that the couple had set for themselves were rather rigid and worked only so long as each spouse stuck to his or her fixed role. When Maggie violated those rules by going to work, Bob was too inflexible to adapt to the change.

In the end, Maggie could not face him and ran away. While one might not have guessed she would react so dramatically, the dissolution of the marriage in some manner was still entirely predictable. Maggie's newfound freedom made divorce desirable, and her independent income made it possible.

Let's be clear on one point, though: In most cases, including this one, a woman's employment is *not* the direct cause of marital dissolution. Rather, the new opportunities for women encourage separation for couples who are already unhappy with their marriages for other reasons. Still, many of these reasons may well involve personal issues intimately related to money, job and career: ambition, competence, industriousness, economic power, higher expectations and exposure to the working world, just to name a few.

How Can Income Differences Trigger Divorce?

It's been known for some time that husbands who earn the least amount of money are most likely to become divorced. Conversely, the higher the income of the husband, the more secure the marriage. The reason: Many men have been conditioned by our culture to feel that it's a mark of male identity to be the main breadwinner for the family. Also, since women generally don't have the same economic potential as men, they may be reluctant to give up a comfortable life style.

But note: Among the very wealthy, this trend is reversed. Great wealth often leads to *more* divorce. Also, rapid change in the state of a family's finances—even positive change—tends to destabilize the marriage.

Andrew Cherlin, a sociologist who has written extensively on the causes and consequences of divorce, has identified another important income- and work-related factor. He argues that the *stability* of the husband's employment, characterized by such factors as fewer layoffs and fewer job changes, may be even more important in protecting against marital dissolution than the actual level of earnings.

Men who do well financially have more stable marriages. But what about women? Surprisingly, the outcome is just the opposite. Women who do not have outside jobs, or who have jobs with small incomes, tend to remain married. Those who make more money, on the other hand, are more likely to divorce. The attitudes toward work outside the home are also important. The greater the wife's commitment to job and career, particularly if that commitment is not shared by her husband, the greater the potential for marital instability.

Another way to digest these facts is to consider the ratio of the husband's earnings to those of his wife, regardless of the actual income level. If the ratio is high, with the man earning the lion's share, domestic peace reigns. When the ratio is low or reversed, where the woman earns the big bucks, domestic strife is the rule. Occasionally, the opposite situation occurs, where the wife may be envious of her husband's greater earning power. But this tends to be the exception rather than the rule.

In general, then, men seem to feel better about themselves when they are bringing home the bacon. Their wives apparently feel better about them too and seem to be more content with their marriages.

Cherlin suggests that the basic threat to family stability is the failure of the father to fulfill the expectations of his family. This makes sense, since of all the social roles a married man must perform, the role of "breadwinner" is perhaps the most significant for his self-esteem and for his family's valuation of him.

In contrast, when women become the economic heavy hitters, their income represents a source of support which is independent of their husbands'—an important consideration for a woman if her love relationship is in trouble. This "independence effect" means that a woman with outside income will be more likely to separate if her marriage is unsatisfactory than a woman without her own funds.

To sum up, then, we don't necessarily advocate that a man must earn more to ensure a stable marriage—just that the partners be aware of the potential consequences when the woman earns more. A *secure* man usually will be thrilled with the economic support, but even the male with the strongest sense of self may have to deal with some feelings of inadequacy. Also, even the strongest wife may experience a touch of anger or fear because her husband "can't take care of me." The best advice is, be prepared!

Some Guidelines for Coping with Economic Differences

Here are a few guidelines that we suggest couples with potential money problems keep in mind. There are plenty of exceptions to these rules, but for most couples, they seem to hold true.

1. IT'S MORE DANGEROUS FOR MEN TO MARRY "UP" ON THE ECONOMIC OR SOCIAL SCALE THAN IT IS FOR WOMEN.

A corollary: Men with modest economic capability should avoid marrying potential female financial superstars.

Such arrangements can work out, but only if both partners enter these relationships with open eyes. The power of the pocketbook is mighty at home, and a husband who makes relatively little can't expect to be the undisputed boss. If you're a man who has to be in charge, you're probably best off marrying a woman who will earn less than you or who will accept a subordinate position.

2. FLEXIBLE MEN MAY BE ABLE TO ADJUST EVEN TO DIFFICULT, THREATENING ECONOMIC REALITIES.

Many husbands who have been laid off from work, for example, have been forced to care for the home and kids, and they find that they like it immensely. These men have been able to redefine their sense of self by assuming such nontraditional male roles as being the primary nurturing parent.

Are you involved with such a flexible man? There will be no way to tell for certain until he's thrust into a situation in which he has to compromise and bend to new pressures. But you can certainly get some idea about where he stands by subtly finding his position on such questions as

- Would it bother you if your wife made more money than you do?
- How would you feel if you lost your job and your wife or someone else had to support you?
- Suppose you and your wife were both up for promotions,

and your wife moved ahead while you didn't. How would that make you feel?
- How do you think money-management responsibilities should be divided around the home?
- Are there some areas of financial responsibility you feel you absolutely must control? If so, what are they? (The more inflexible a person is about this kind of issue, the more at risk the marriage will be in time of economic crisis.)
- Do you think men are naturally more gifted with money than women? (If the answer is "yes," be careful!)

The main idea here is not to conduct a police-style interrogation of your partner, but rather to check out his overall philosophy on family finances, including the extent to which he can be flexible in changing times. Also, you want to be sure that he'll be supportive of you if you should feel a need to shift your own career aspirations.

3. MOST WOMEN WANT THEIR MEN TO BE AMBITIOUS.

When the man isn't ambitious, the relationship is less likely to last beyond the first few years. For traditional women, particularly those with expensive tastes, men who would rather garden or paint than work are high-risk marital partners. Far from competing for economic dominance, these couples end up quarreling about his lack of industriousness and the chronic shortage of money. Such a man may be acceptable for the woman who can accept a very simple, impecunious life, but can be a disaster for one who wants upward mobility and financial success.

4. MANY SUCCESSFUL MEN THRIVE ON DYNAMIC PROFESSIONAL WIVES— AT LEAST INITIALLY.

The men in these situations seem to love the stimulation and excitement, and these marriages often work out quite well in the early years. But before you decide such marriages are ideal, we should tell you that our experience shows that in the long run, they can be riskier than traditional unions.

For one thing, remorse and frustration can emerge because both husbands and wives must give up notions of being full-time parents. These spouses must frequently recruit others to help with the children, then deal with the guilt of not meeting the parenting standards of their own parents.

Also, complex schedules must be worked out and agreed upon, with compromises required on everything from where to live to when to have sex. Those kinds of demands can place undue pressure on any marriage. It's important to talk these issues out as much as possible in advance of the wedding date, just to be sure you have a basic agreement and plan for juggling career and family responsibilities.

5. IT'S IMPORTANT TO ASCERTAIN WHETHER THE WOMAN REALLY WANTS TO WORK, OR WHETHER SHE WILL ENTER THE JOB MARKET ONLY OUT OF NECESSITY.

Many women today work not by choice, but out of sheer economic necessity. Some of these wives may well resent their husbands for not earning enough to keep them at home. Others, though, will blossom in their newfound independent careers.

Because the future economic circumstances of any marriage are uncertain, we recommend that those women who plan on not working at least assume a flexible attitude toward work. That way, they will be better prepared to deal with resentments that may arise if hard times arrive. As for men, it's best that they select a partner who is open to the idea of work, just in case that becomes a necessity.

All guidelines and rules aside, people do change with time, and so do marriages. A husband can't assume that even the most conventional-seeming wife will tend the house forever. And a wife must recognize that the most ambitious-seeming husband may grow sick of the rat race, come middle age. At the beginning of a relationship, men may advocate traditional roles; they may *say* they want their wives to stay at home. But then they may become less traditional over time; they may feel angry or frustrated at their wives for "doing nothing" in a financial crunch, or after the kids grow older.

In any event, everyone should have a backup skill to hedge against unexpected economic change. Rigidity makes for a high divorce risk, particularly when neither partner can adapt to changing circumstances. The capacity for flexibility in at least one spouse lowers the divorce risk considerably.

SIXTEEN

How Do You Talk, Fight and Make Decisions?

The importance of communication is so obvious that to mention it may seem almost trite, but don't allow the sometimes hackneyed nature of this issue to fool you into downplaying it. In fact, a proven predictor of ultimate marital success is the effectiveness with which the partners listen and talk to each other *before* the wedding.

What's Your Style of Communication?

Someone once calculated that the average American couple spends fifteen minutes a day speaking to one another in edifying, relationship-enhancing conversation. From our practical experience with couples whose marriages are in some sort of trouble, we'd have to agree that this estimate is accurate.

How can two people who have spent all day and half the night talking on the phone when they were courting become so uncommunicative? In fact, most couples do engage in some sort of verbal communication more than fifteen minutes a day, but in many cases, those words pull the marriage down, rather than build it up. Here are a few of the most destructive ways that language in marriage may do more damage than many spouses realize.

ARGUING.

Arguing, as we're using the term here, must be distinguished from fighting, which we'll discuss shortly.

In brief, the distinction goes like this: The arguer can execute his verbal or intellectual attack on the other person dispassionately, without the slightest trace of rancor or anger. (That is, there's no anger in the person launching the assault, though the target of the argument may certainly become angry or hurt.) Fighting, in contrast, involves stronger, more hostile emotions on the part of both people who are engaged in the verbal combat.

This couple's experience illustrates what we mean when we refer to the classic arguer:

Randy is a successful criminal lawyer in his late thirties, and Jayne is an artist, a few years younger. Randy loves to talk and spar verbally, and his closing arguments have become legendary for their convincing power, if not their length. Unfortunately, though, he tries to apply his courtroom techniques at home.

Jayne doesn't enjoy the verbal jousting that is central to Randy's life. She is much more at ease with friendly conversation, no conflict, and a silent canvas. Though just as bright and creative as her husband, she prefers the inner dialogue of her own mind. When a disagreement breaks out, Randy may exult in crafting clever phrases and scoring points against her, but Jayne just feels outgunned and emotionally violated.

Randy used to win most of the arguments at home, but now he wins all of them—by default. When he starts to talk, Jayne just clams up. Randy realizes that something is seriously wrong and that his victories are hollow; consequently, he becomes frustrated and angry. Furthermore, he feels neglected and ignored. He came to us for help in extricating him from this verbal dilemma in which he had become trapped.

After several weeks of counseling, Randy has learned that he must restrain himself and keep from overwhelming his wife. Otherwise, they'll never get a decent conversation going again. He has great difficulty not pulling out his prodigious verbal weapons. Yet every time he does, Jayne retreats and in effect creates a stalemate by shutting him out.

Our suggestion to Randy: For a two-week period, lay your argumentative style aside and just *listen* to Jayne. As excruciating as it may be for you, let her have the last word in any decisions that come up. Above all, don't engage in verbal battle!

We explained that this complete reversal of communication style can sometimes break a pattern of being "stuck" at a behavioral impasse. Then, when the dialogue between partners begins to flow again, the more forceful, verbal partner can tentatively begin to be more assertive once more.

In this case, the strategy worked. Jayne was disconcerted at first, but after a day or so, she began to take the lead in initiating conversations and in decision making. She was wary of Randy for about a week, but then the flow of their conversation became more natural again.

At the end of the two-week period, Randy became more assertive, and once again he ran into defensiveness from Jayne when he came on too strong. But now he felt more comfortable backing off into his more passive approach until the free flow of conversation began again.

NAGGING.

Nagging presents somewhat different problems. Peter, a classic nagger, typically repeated himself in conversations with his wife Miriam, who never seemed able to do anything to his satisfaction. Because he knew somehow that he was frequently being obnoxious, he tried to restrain himself at times. In many discussions, though, he could never seem to hold his tongue.

When this couple entered marital therapy, they behaved true

to form. Miriam sat morosely, while Peter droned on, cataloging all the things she had done wrong during the week. He addressed most of his complaints to the therapist.

"Doctor," he said, "she promised to clean up the laundry room, but she still hasn't done it. She was supposed to meet me at the restaurant earlier today, and she came twenty minutes late. She's always late. She gets that from her mother, who is also inconsiderate."

The therapist's mind soon began to wander, and he gazed out the window—only to become the target of the nagging himself.

"Doctor," Peter said sternly, mispronouncing his name. "I hope you understand what I'm getting at here. After all, we are paying for your time. Now, try this on for size: Miriam always tells me that I'm nagging, but I have a theory that goes back to some of her childhood experiences. . . ."

This interchange presented the therapist with a perfect opportunity to show Peter how he had fallen into the habit of browbeating other people, including the therapist himself. Usually, the person who is the victim of the nagging or browbeating will finally withdraw, either emotionally or physically, from the relationship. That's what Miriam had done.

Unlike the wife, the therapist confronted Peter with what he was doing. "You may seem to end up the 'winner' in these discussions because your wife just becomes quiet," the therapist said. "But in fact, that's a hollow victory because the 'loser,' your wife, isn't really a loser at all. She's simply stopped playing your game."

In general, though, withdrawal by one partner doesn't solve the problem. The nagger will just continue with the destructive behavior and either make life miserable for the other person, or force him or her to leave the relationship and perhaps get a divorce.

The therapist's approach is a better way to handle most naggers: Confront them openly with what they are doing every time they launch into a browbeating mode, then refuse to play the game until the nagging stops. One husband used this approach with his nagging wife: "Okay, now you're starting to nag. You've said it once, and that's all I need to hear. I've got the message. Now, is there anything else?"

If the nagger is sensitive to his or her partner's needs and wants to strengthen the relationship, he or she will back off. If not, outside help may be required.

FIGHTING.

Most couples argue from time to time, and those who do not have probably given up on on each other long ago. The great psychoanalyst Erik Erikson once said that the inability to engage in "controversy and useful combat" is indicative of a lack of human intimacy.

Arguing is a normal, indeed a necessary part of married life. Some couples thrive on verbal sparring and may not feel "alive" unless the juices of combat flow periodically. Furthermore, these happy battlers may have as high a Compatibility Quotient as anyone else.

On the other hand, a really nasty temper or a tendency to deal in dirty tactics or personal attacks during a fight can increase the vulnerability to divorce. Honest, intense communication is fine, and expressions of anger are all right in small and restrained doses. But frequent yelling, screaming or verbal abuse is dangerous to the stability of a married pair.

EXCESSIVE SILENCE.

The Compatibility Quotient is also low when two people can't seem to find anything to talk about when they are alone. They may do quite well in crowds, but conversation may seem to screech to a halt when they find themselves face-to-face with each other, without the buffer of friends and acquaintances.

Calvin told us that he thought that he and Mary Beth had a basically good relationship. "We're interested in the same things, and the sex is great. We like each other's friends. But we never spent any long periods of time together until this latest vacation was thrust on us.

"Then we went to a secluded island in the Bahamas. It was

beautiful, with a perfect sunset and all that. An hour after we got there, though, Mary Beth and I ran out of things to say. We spent the rest of the weekend pretty quiet, not angry, just nothing to talk about. Even sex wasn't enough after a while."

It may be that these two young people just needed time to get to know each other and conquer their shyness. But that's unlikely, given the fact that they had reached such a close stage of physical intimacy with one another. It's more likely that their inability to converse naturally is a signal that there's something basically wrong with their relationship.

In this particular case, there wasn't anything wrong with either person's personality or intelligence. They just happened not to be that drawn to one another. Their physical infatuation had now faded, and they found that there is little basis for a continuing relationship. As a result, they have been advised to postpone marriage until they both become convinced that their attachment is, quite literally, more than skin deep.

None of these problems—arguing, nagging, fighting or silence—may be a major factor in your relationship. But *every* marriage contains some sort of conflict, with the accompanying need to resolve that conflict in a way that will strengthen rather than damage the tie.

The Challenge of Conflict

In every marriage, a basic state of tension exists between the need for intimacy and the need for separateness. The balance between closeness and privacy must be continually renegotiated by the couple. Finding the proper balance is often a source of friction and may be reflected in such common complaints as, "He never wants to do things together," or, "She's always sticking her nose in my business."

During arguments over such tensions, women tend to be pursuers and men, distancers. When there are problems, men typically withdraw and become more removed, while women coerce or placate. In addition, men are often oblivious to anger in their wives and avoid confrontation, while women are more sensitive to trouble. Women are also more facile at switching from a hostile to a conciliatory stance, and in ending the fight. Note: These gender patterns do *not* seem to change with changing times. There's an ongoing consistency about the way men and women are socialized: Men are conditioned to be independent and self-sufficient, and women to nurture and please others.

On the other hand, the reverse may be true in certain families. The woman may withdraw, and the man will try to make up. It really doesn't matter who takes which role, so long as the conflicts are addressed. When both spouses withdraw, though, nothing ever seems to get resolved.

In resolving conflicts in a marriage equitably, it's important to observe the principle of being *responsive*, rather than reactive. If you are responsive, you hear your spouse out, listening carefully to what he or she has to say. Then, you think about what's been said and respond with your own views. Finally, the two of you work out a mutually agreeable solution.

Reactivity involves more of a knee-jerk reply to problems. In this situation, listening takes a backseat because it requires effort to try to understand how someone else feels. It's much easier to react automatically, without much thought, and vent anger or displeasure indiscriminately.

Some typical variations of reactivity:

THE DEFENSIVE WIFE.

Howard says his wife cries when he criticizes her family. "Usually, I'm completely objective and I'm not trying to put her folks down," he told us. "I love them! But she always takes everything so personally."

THE EXPLOSIVE HUSBAND.

Sally told us, "Sometimes, when Burt comes home at night, I'm scared to death to tell him that anything went wrong in my life during the day. More often than not, he just flies off the handle at me and tells me he doesn't know why I have to unload my troubles on him when he's trying to forget the pressures of the office."

THE STRESSED-OUT SPOUSE.

Alice gave this account of her husband's reaction to tension: "I remember when I had this little fender bender last year. I called my husband at his office and told him that our elderly neighbor hadn't been looking when he pulled out of his garage, and he backed into my car. I had all I could do to keep Mike from leaving work and punching the poor old guy in the jaw!"

In each of these situations, one spouse is having particular difficulty resolving the conflicts or tensions in his or her life. All too often, the tendency is to take out the frustration and anger on someone else—often the other partner in the relationship.

Before you get involved seriously with another person, it's essential to determine how he or she approaches tensions and conflicts, and resolves them. If your partner is inept in this area, it's likely that you will eventually become the target of his or her inner turmoil. To get an idea about how your partner handles the resolution of conflicts and tensions answer these questions:

- Does she hear you out and respond rationally and calmly to difficult situations, or does she react emotionally and quickly?
- When you raise a touchy issue, does he hear you out and display a willingness to work with you and perhaps negotiate? Or does he typically get angry or rigid, and perhaps go on the offensive before you even get a chance to finish speaking?
- When you say you're displeased by something your partner has said or done, does she immediately become defensive or go on the attack?

The way a couple deals with conflict and tension tends to be the same after the wedding as it was before. If you find that your partner doesn't listen to you now, or belittles you, or is thick-headed and stubborn, those traits are not likely to change very easily.

If you're already married to a person who is more of a reacter than a responder, you'll be faced with the formidable task of trying to work with him and help change the patterns of conversation that have developed in your relationship. The best chance of success lies in your ability to identify the source of your mate's problem, then to encourage him or her to "put it on the table" and discuss it in depth.

Most likely, there will be some emotional interchanges as you go through this process, and if the conversation gets too heated, or if you find you've reached a dead end, bringing in a dispassionate friend as a kind of third-party mediator may be helpful. Otherwise, professional therapy may be in order.

How to Predict the Decision-Making Potential in a Marriage

Power is a vital concept in every relationship because marriages can become stable only as a balance of power emerges between the partners. Perhaps the most common way for this balance of power to be expressed is in the decision-making process.

POWER IN THE EGALITARIAN MARRIAGE.

Ideally, each spouse should share power and decision making in relatively equal portions. Of course, that doesn't mean that every decision must be voted on by both. A division of labor is fine, and partners frequently take turns being in charge of different duties. Still, it's necessary for there to be at least a tacit agreement about who controls what and how most decisions are going to be made.

There are two basic kinds of power in a marriage. The more obvious one is the power of the purse, which translates into who decides where the couple lives and what it spends. Equally important is emotional power, the ability of each partner to strengthen and comfort the other. Egalitarian arrangements strike a balance of power or, in the words of social researcher Francine Klagsbrun, a "balance of dependencies."

We personally prefer egalitarian marriages. In fact, we like to think that we ourselves have one, though each of us feels browbeaten by the other from time to time. We recognize, however, that there are other ways of sharing power that are equally conducive to stabilizing a marriage, if not more so.

POWER IN THE TRADITIONAL MARRIAGE.

Consider, for example, the stereotype of the "traditional marriage." The man appears to be the boss, but everyone knows that the woman is the "power behind the throne." This usually means that the husband wields the economic strength, but the emotional power belongs to the wife. He can bluster about, pronounce judgments and issue orders. But when he finally runs out of steam, it's the woman who comforts him and whispers in his ear the course of action that would really be the most constructive.

THE DANGER OF THE TYRANT.

A problem arises, however when one spouse consistently dominates the other and refuses to relinquish any control over decision making. The weaker mate may chafe for years under this sort of authoritarian rule, often becoming too immobilized by his or her sense of helplessness to do much about it.

These marriages survive as little more than empty shells because the partners have chosen, for a variety of reasons, to avoid divorce. The apparent stability is illusory, however. Given the opportunity, the weaker partner is liable to pull the ultimate power play and walk out.

Along these lines, we saw a "runaway housewife" several years ago. She was a devout Roman Catholic who had been married to a tyrant for more than thirty years. Her husband was never physically abusive, but this woman was little more than his well-kept housekeeper.

Then, when the youngest of her six sons was grown, she suddenly left home and moved in with a group of nuns. Though nearing sixty, she went to work as a typist in a Catholic agency. She rejected financial support from her wealthy husband; her only desire was to avoid any contact at all with him.

"What about your religion?" we asked.

"Catholicism stands for human freedom, not slavery," she said. "Now, I'm free. I don't need a divorce to prove it."

True joint decision making can never take place in this sort of relationship, and in most cases, the marriage will collapse.

THE IMPORTANCE OF NEGOTIATION.

One of the best ways to determine whether your prospective mate will share decision making with you is to test that person's ability and inclination to negotiate with you. Among other things, you should check whether your partner will share both large and small decisions with you, and also whether he or she is able to compromise.

Lance talked a good line about equality, but Jody decided she would put him to the test. She suggested that they plan a party together, with the decision-making functions shared between them. Very quickly, problems began to emerge.

Jody wanted to invite only the closest friends and few relatives. Lance wanted all their friends and the people he worked with, but he declared relatives to be off limits.

"You're a grown-up now," he said rather condescendingly. "You're no longer tied to your mother's apron strings."

"I just thought I'd like her to join us at the party," Jody replied, somewhat shaken by his angry, sarcastic reaction.

Jody also thought the party should be held at her apartment, but Lance insisted on his club. Jody thought it should be on Friday night; Lance wanted Sunday afternoon. And so it went.

The couple finally hammered out a compromise of sorts, but each thought that he or she had given up too much. The planning disputes were minor, though, compared to the problems that lay ahead.

More of Jody's friends came than Lance's, and Lance thought the bill for the gathering should be divided in proportion to the number of guests. Jody accused him of stinginess and suggested that the charge be split equally. When they couldn't resolve the issue, Lance whipped out his checkbook and in a huff declared that he would foot the whole bill.

During the actual festivities the conflict continued. Jody wanted to be a gracious hostess, so she tried to talk to all the guests, men as well as women. But Lance accused her of flirting with the men.

Jody felt that Lance spent too much time with his buddies discussing business.

After the party was over, Lance apologized for being so difficult, but to one degree or another, a similar reaction occurred every time the couple planned to do anything together. As a result, Jody eventually ended the relationship.

"Sure, he's always sorry," she told us. "He acts like an idiot and apologizes, but that's not the point.

"Everything is always fine when we talk about the kind of married life we'll have. But I learned that in the real world, we just can't work together."

A good way to discover the actual power distribution in your relationship is to plan several projects before you marry. You might try a shared all-day outing with another couple or two, or a large dinner. Then, you'll be forced to negotiate your differences and deal with your respective feelings. Each of you will learn how well you work together, how you spend money and how you handle disagreements.

During these joint ventures, you should answer questions like these:

- Can each partner make his or her wishes clear to the other?
- Is there respect toward what each person thinks?
- Does your partner feel that he or she alone has "the truth"?
- Does your friend attribute malevolent impulses to your innocent mistakes?
- Is there an attempt to coerce you, rather than compromise?
- How well does the other person accept criticism?
- Does he or she complain excessively, even if things are really going pretty well?
- How similar are your views about spending money?

The way you make decisions in a joint project will tell you a great deal about your probability of negotiating successfully in a long-term relationship. You may not always be pleased by what you learn, but at least you'll end up with a better estimate of your Compatibility Quotient.

SEVENTEEN

The Risk
of Remarriage

People who remarry have a higher divorce rate than first-timers. Why should remarriage carry such risks? In part, the statistics showing greater risk in remarriage are skewed because some people are "divorcers." That is, they are chronically unable to stay married very long and end up going from partner to partner.

But the danger can't be explained completely by these chronic divorcers. A second marriage failure may also occur because of one or more of these common risk factors:

- An unknowing tendency to repeat mistakes of the past
- The haunting of the present marriage by the ghosts of the past marriage
- Turmoil created by the presence of stepchildren
- Various money messes

Risk 1: The Repetition of Past Mistakes

The single greatest risk in marrying again is repeating the same mistakes. This is a real danger because we are all controlled to some degree by unconscious forces that don't change much over the course of a lifetime. In other words, many of the same impulses that caused you to marry your first spouse will influence your choice of the second. The end result: Your new mate may be a carbon copy of the last one.

Earl's Second Chance

Earl was widowed after he turned fifty. His first marriage, to Liz, was a twenty-year disaster because, it was rumored, Liz had drunk herself to death. She also had been an overbearing woman, discontented and demanding. Earl, a peace-loving sort, had dealt with her nonstop criticisms by lapsing into almost total silence.

Shortly after Liz's death, Earl met and married Betty, a divorcee who was an almost exact duplicate of his first wife, except that she didn't have the serious drinking problem. Everyone who had known Liz remarked on the similarity of the two women, even down to their physical resemblance. Betty was also a nonstop talking machine, and Earl became even quieter than ever.

As they settled into their marriage, Betty began to accuse Earl of being rigid and withholding, and of driving his first wife to drink. Eventually, frustrated that her critique of his personal flaws didn't seem to be getting through to him, she delivered an ultimatum: She warned Earl that unless he changed, she would leave him—just as she had left her first husband, who also had never been willing to change.

In response, Earl became depressed. If he could have figured out how to change his ways, he would have been willing. He was an accommodating person. But no matter how hard he tried, his efforts never seemed to satisfy Betty, as they had failed to satisfy Liz.

In fact, Earl had come to believe it was his fate to live with overbearing women. For her part, Betty started to assume that she was doomed to relationships with silent men. They finally went in for some marriage counseling, but by the time they sought professional counseling, it was too late. Soon, Betty initiated divorce proceedings, and now the legal separation is final.

What was the underlying cause of this failure?

Earl recalled with pain the way his mother always screamed at him and his father, whose failure to react enraged the mother even more. Earl, following his father's example, also learned to withdraw into an emotional shell when his mother attacked. Although he swore that he would never marry an angry screamer, he did precisely that—twice!

As for Betty, she took the cue from her mother, who had been domineering in her relationship with a quiet, unassertive husband. Betty's mother constantly berated her spouse for his perceived inadequacies, such as his inability to earn as much money as she wanted or to secure promotions which she believed would have raised her social status. The father, who was the main male figure in Betty's life, was weak, and the main female authority figure, her mother, was overwhelmingly strong. This family pattern was all Betty knew, so it was easy for her to repeat it in her two failed marriages.

There is a human tendency to seek out that which is familiar—even when the familiar is destructive and undesirable. Sigmund Freud called this phenomenon the "repetition compulsion," an apt description for the pattern into which Earl and Betty had fallen.

What could Earl or Betty have done differently? The best answer to this question is probably this: They should have identified and learned from their former mistakes, and avoided blaming the former spouse.

When people in the process of divorce attempt to analyze what has gone wrong, they almost always focus on the flaws in the former spouse. The ex must be downgraded to reassure the other partner that what has happened to the marriage is really for the best. The legal process, in particular, encourages blame. Feeling genuinely self-righteous makes it easier for a person to make tough demands in court.

After the dust has settled, however, the time comes for the

blaming to taper off. Each person should finally understand the part he or she has played in the divorce and be willing to accept responsibility for it. This is not a question of fairness, but rather of emotional and relational health. Those who divorce but have no idea why it happened will marry and divorce again, and again, and perhaps again. Yet they'll never understand. Knowledge is the key to overcoming the risk of remarriage and raising the Compatibility Quotient.

Risk 2: The Ghosts of Relationships Past

All remarriages have ghosts, the unseen but controlling presences of the former spouse, in-laws or other people and situations. Sometimes these memories seem pleasant and positive; other times, they are negative. But in practically every case, the ghosts increase the risk of divorce—especially if they are carryover impressions from a spouse who has died.

Widowed people, such as Earl, frequently feel that their former mate is watching from the grave. Yet the impression is frozen in time, either as an unchangeable negative presence or as a hopelessly idealized image, because the dead person is no longer around.

One remarried woman, Carla, told us, "I love Gene [her current spouse], but the fact is, I would still be married to Chester if he hadn't died."

Gene had too much to live up to in this marriage. He was constantly being compared with Chester, and the comparisons were always unfavorable. It was only after several months of counseling that Carla was able to release her memories of Chester.

One of the ways we helped her achieve this objective was to encourage her to be realistic about her former husband: What mistakes did he make? What were his shortcomings and personal flaws?

When Carla could confront these negatives and plug them into her total recollections of Chester, she was better able to appreciate the strengths and good qualities of Gene. Only then could she begin to live in the present, rather than always injecting her idealized former husband as a third "spouse" into the current relationship.

It's quite true that widows and widowers don't choose to leave their former marriage. But because the death was an event beyond their control, they mistakenly assume that they have no right to complain about their former spouse, even if the marriage wasn't all that great. Consequently, they are often inhibited in talking about the old marriage with the new spouse.

The only cure for these ghosts of relationships past, then, is exorcism: Realistic analysis of the old marriage and sensitive discussions with the new spouse about the former marriage can greatly reduce this risk.

Specters may also plague second marriages in the form of disputes over old homes, where one of the original families once lived. For this reason, we recommend that an all-out effort be made to move to a new house or apartment, where neither family has a carryover history of experiences and relationships.

Consider the commonsense basis for this advice. There's nothing very romantic, for example, about sleeping in your new mate's original marital bed. Nor does it help your current relationship to hear, "We always ate breakfast over there." Or, "Sam taught the kids to skate on that walk." Overall, it's simply impossible to purge an old home of all the emotional residue of the former marriage.

Also, when a new mate moves in with children from the old marriage, there is bound to be some competition and probably rage that wells up in the resident kids, who now find they have to share their living space with the "interlopers." The new kids will likely be angry and resentful because this home is not really theirs. For a number of reasons, then, staying in a spouse's former home is a prescription for trouble.

Risk 3: The Presence of Stepchildren

Another great risk to remarital stability is the presence of children from the former marriage. Furthermore, if both mates come with kids, the risks are even higher.

Many of the reasons for this danger are quite obvious. He may love her, but he may not love her kids. She may think his children are fine, but she cannot deal with the way his ex-wife treats the kids. When pressures from problems involving stepchildren become too great, the message that may come across is, "Choose me or choose your children."

When both mates bring children to the marriage, there is often the unspoken hope of creating an instant "extended family." This dream is usually doomed to failure. The couple will most likely end up with a different kind of family, but not one that is a new or better version of the old one. Even where the mix is fairly good among the spouses and kids, expectations must be modest. The fun and harmony of the idealized "Brady Bunch" of television fame rarely occurs in real life, at least not right away.

Another potential problem is that your children may not like the partner you've picked. Perhaps the chemistry is wrong, or the relationship just needs time to mature. Children should not be expected to share their parents' happiness or to accept the new mate automatically as a parent. Their problem may not be with your new spouse at all, but rather, with a feeling of disloyalty to the parent who is not there.

Stepsibling interactions are another common source of trouble. These also are frequently marked by loyalty conflicts. Each set of children in the "reconstituted" family predated the new marriage, and each possesses a unique history. Well-meaning attempts to ignore the differences, rather than to discuss them and respect them, will undermine the stability of the new marriage.

Under the best of circumstances, it takes about two years for a stepparent and stepchildren to find ways to get along. Even then, the relationship may be no more than an uneasy truce. Sometimes the situation works out pretty quickly, but you should not go into remarriage expecting that your kids and your new mate will be fast friends. Stepparents don't take the place of anyone—they are an addition. Moreover, unrealistic expectations decrease compatibility because there is bound to be disappointment.

Will and Ginny's New Family

Will, a high school teacher, was deserted by his wife when his son, Bryan, was only four. Shortly afterwards, he dated Ginny, an old friend who recently had been divorced. Ginny had been left with a four-year-old daughter, Becca.

Will and Ginny married after twelve months, when their children were both five. In the view of many friends, this seemed a match made in heaven. The couple appeared to be well suited for one another, and the kids were young enough not to have acquired the emotional baggage that can be so disruptive with older stepchildren.

The couple did live together happily for a number of years, but they were still plagued by ghosts of the old relationships and by feelings about the children that threatened evenhanded treatment.

Will didn't talk about his first wife for many years. It was too painful, and Ginny elected not to pry. Will also changed the subject whenever Ginny tried to talk about her former husband. After a while, though, Will's refusal to confront his or her past began to bother Ginny immensely. She had a great need to open up and deal with the hurt and rejection she felt. Also, she wanted to be reassured that Will really accepted and loved her, at least as much as he had his former wife. But Will wasn't eager to talk.

From outward appearances, the two were fine parents, and one would have had to look long and hard to find any evidence of favoritism. But the walls that Will encouraged in the relationship caused Ginny to be protective toward her own daughter, sometimes at the expense of Bryan.

"I loved Will's son from the beginning," Ginny told us. "He has never known another mother, and I have never been a step-anything to him. In many ways, we have been as close as most mothers and sons, I suppose.

"But still, all in all, there was a difference. I know I haven't given Bryan all of myself. Becca was my child and Bryan was Will's. The truth is that I loved Becca more and gave her more of my time, and the situation has gotten worse as the children have grown older. I guess I've felt that since Will wouldn't let me entirely into his life, he wouldn't let Becca in either. So I sort of had to make up the difference. I just hope none of this has been apparent to Bryan."

Ginny came to see us because she and Will had been growing steadily more distant from each other, even though she was pregnant with another child. She feared that this third youngster might push their relationship over the edge and cause them to head for a divorce.

Her willingness to take steps to save the marriage came in time, however. Her best decision was that she accepted her husband's unwillingness to talk about his past and became more sympathetic about the great pain that prevented him from being as open as she could be. This very refusal to push him helped draw them closer together.

Also, as she told us after the birth of the new baby, "Maybe the best thing that could have happened to us was the birth of Joey. Everyone, including the children, immediately loved him without reservations. No one felt disloyal or protective about him. Becca and Bryan—especially Bryan—assumed parentlike roles with Joey, and that helped me overcome any walls I may have erected between myself and Bryan."

In some ways, then, little Joey became the central focus in this family, the force that was able to help hold everything together and make the marriage work.

Unfortunately, though, most remarried couples with children are far more burdened than this one. Take scheduling of visits by ex-spouses, for instance. One woman and her ex share custody of their three children. The kids are at her house four days and at his house for three.

To complicate matters further, this woman's new husband has visitation rights for his own two children; he sees them on alternate weekends and every Wednesday night.

With these arrangements, there are countless permutations of who is where, and at what time. A weekend free of any children is a rarity. Unlike first-timers, then, remarried couples must work extra hard to make the time and space to be alone together. If they fail to find time for themselves, their marital risks rise considerably.

Note: Adolescents are a special problem. For one thing, they may not get along. Even touchier, perhaps, is the situation in which a boy and girl from different families live under the same roof and get along *too* well. To make matters worse, there are no incest taboos to keep young people apart in this situation.

Risk 4: Money Messes

Every successful remarriage is founded on a delicate mixture of love and hardheaded, dollars-and-cents reality. The reason for the importance of practical matters like money management is that the second time around, things are not as simple as they were the first time.

The main challenge the first time was breaking away from parents and shaping an independent life as a couple. But with a remarriage, you must add the complication of shedding the remnants of a failed marriage. One of the most difficult of these complications is working out new financial arrangements.

Remarried families are often strapped for funds. Not uncommonly, the new husband is paying some sort of maintenance to his former family, as well as assuming support for his new wife and her children. Working out child support arrangements is always a problem, particularly with the many novel modes of sharing custody that are now practiced.

As a result, the two new spouses should both be aware of *all* the financial implications of entering into the new marriage. This calls for a lengthy discussion about the *exact* amount of money that will be available to live on, and the legal ties and obligations that each spouse has with the ex-spouse. Accompany such discussions by taking notes and making calculations so that you can make decisions about your future with some precision. Here are some issues to keep in mind in this type of discussion:

• Do I need a prenuptial agreement? These contracts are quite common when people marry for the second time, especially when one or both spouses want to ensure that existing funds will continue to be available for children (e.g., for college education).

- How much financial responsibility will my new spouse's ex-spouse assume for his children—and how reliable is he in meeting his obligations?
- What are the child support arrangements that my spouse has entered into, and what effect will these provisions have on me and my children, in terms of time as well as money?
- Do any children in my family or my spouse's have access to separate funds? If so, what is the possibility that resentments may arise between children who have less money than their stepsiblings?

As with other aspects of remarriage, these and other issues over money won't go away if you ignore them. Potential conflicts *must* be worked out through in-depth discussions so that no family member feels cheated. Financial arrangements should be designed as much as possible to minimize envy in the children and to build a feeling of family unity.

Successful remarriage is quite possible, of course. In fact, many second and even third marriages may be even better than first marriages. Through luck or insight gained as a result of hard experience, the divorced man or woman may make a better choice—or have learned to be a better mate—the second time around. But remarriage, perhaps more than any other situation, places a high premium on each partner's entering the relationship with no illusions.

EIGHTEEN

You Can Only Change Yourself

Jamie, a devout Baptist, had been involved in unending conflict with his wife, a woman whom he deeply loved but who constantly frustrated him. He thought she was a flirt and an excessive spender. He rarely said anything to her about his discontent, though; he just pouted in angry silence.

For her part, Suzanne was totally put off by Jamie's stony silence. She had no idea about what, if anything, she had done wrong. Because he seemed unwilling to talk to her about what was going on inside him, she felt confronted by an unresponsive brick wall and wondered if their marriage was really going to make it.

Jamie met with us several times, but we failed initially to convince him to begin opening up to his wife. He listened closely to our advice but responded, "I'll think about it and see if I can find a way to convince her that there's a problem. And I'll pray about it."

Jamie insisted that he saw prayer as the ultimate answer to this dilemma, as he did every other problem in his life. We encouraged him to continue with this discipline, even as he tried to open up his relationship with his wife in other ways.

As he told us later, he prayed day and night for his wife to change, but nothing happened. Then, he began to despair and even to question his faith. But he redoubled his efforts at prayer, and finally he experienced a breakthrough.

The next day, he appeared at our office obviously content and peaceful, the exact opposite of the unhappy, worried man we had been dealing with before.

"Did the prayer work?" he asked.

"Yes, it did," he replied. "God always answers prayer. But not always in the way we expect."

We look at him in puzzlement. "What happened?"

"You see, all these months I've prayed that my wife would change her ways, but nothing ever happened. She just went on doing what she always did.

"So I prayed even more, and then at last the answer came. It suddenly dawned on me that our problems are at least half *my* fault and maybe more. Yet I've been doing nothing to correct them.

"I came to realize that I've always been a mama's boy. My mother loved me without reservation, perhaps too much, and she anticipated my every need. I never had to say anything to her; she knew intuitively what I wanted and provided me with it. But my wife is different. She loves me deeply too, but she doesn't try to anticipate my needs that way, and she won't coax me or baby me."

Then Jamie wrapped up his story: "I always knew that if you pray for something, you'll get it. God always gives you what is good for you.

"I had asked the Lord to change my wife, and He made me realize that it was I who had to change. Also, He showed me that it's perfectly within my power to do so. Now I'm going to let my wife know more about what's going on inside me, and I'll look for ways to improve myself. Then, I know the right kind of change will result in our marriage."

So Jamie opened up and confessed his own shortcomings, then

told his wife what he needed from her to make him happy. She was quite eager to provide what he asked.

Also, his openness made her feel free to tell him how enraged she had become at his passivity. As a result, Jamie became more active and assertive in the relationship.

We don't know if they lived happily ever after, but their marriage certainly seems to be back on the right track—all because one partner realized that the first and most important change had to be wrought in himself, rather than in his mate.

A Matter of Expectations

Whether a marriage succeeds or not is often dependent on the nature of the couple's premarital expectations about the possibility of change. For one thing, if one partner enters the marriage expecting to work fundamental changes in the other, this hope is doomed to failure. Also, if one expects the other to meet all of his or her needs, this dream is also bound to remain unfulfilled.

Exaggerated expectations about the possibility of changing a partner are often based on comic book illusions of romantic love. These inflated hopes will inhibit genuine attempts to negotiate a solution to the problems in a new marriage—and will always lead to disappointment.

Expectations are sometimes very unrealistic and destructive, even in the best of marriages. One's expectations often come from internalized images taken from childhood. Everyone harbors secret hopes and images of what marriage will accomplish.

Unfortunately, though, the realities of married life rarely live up to our fondest illusions and hidden agendas. To be successful, couples must be willing to give up their illusions, or at least accommodate them to the realities of the partner and the situation.

How can you identify your illusions about marriage? We recommend that first of all, you set aside a few minutes to contemplate your special notions and fantasies about marriage. Picture your *ideal* spouse—and how he or she looks, acts and relates to you. Then, compare this ideal with your real-life partner. What discrepancies do you perceive between the reality and the ideal?

Most likely, those discrepancies reflect the essence of your illusions about marriage. When you're ready to give up the illusions, you'll find true compatibility a more attainable goal.

The Promise of Change

The Compatibility Quotient is not a fixed or immutable thing. To some extent, all human beings are capable of change, and we've seen couples' CQs go up when the partners are willing to work on their relationships. What's involved in such beneficial change? At least three important realizations:

CHANGE TAKES WORK.

It isn't easy to alter habits that have taken years to acquire. Children certainly don't like to change their ways, and adults are even more resistant. It's much easier just to run away. A patient put it rather well when he was about to leave a relationship that had become uncomfortably intense: "When the going gets rough, I'm ready to get going!"

CHANGE CAN AFFECT BEHAVIOR AND BELIEF.

Even if we cannot change our fundamental personalities, we can all change the way we act. If we wish to, we can become more tolerant, less stubborn, or more receptive to the needs of the person we love. None of these behavior alterations involves a total personality transplant! More often than not, only a marginal change in your behavior is quite enough.

YOU CAN ONLY CHANGE YOURSELF.

This is the most important realization of all—the one Jamie arrived at after prayer. There's probably nothing you can do to change the person you're involved with. That's up to that individual, not you. But up to a point, you can change yourself. You can alter your own behavior—especially your negative, destructive behavior—if you're willing to do so.

There's a side benefit: If you're successful in changing for the better, the other person will often follow suit.

So, as you consider the degree of compatibility you now have with your partner, always remember that some elevation of that Compatibility Quotient may be possible—*if* you are willing to begin with yourself. In love as well as in other relationships, we must first learn to remove the log from our own eye before we begin to tinker with the splinter in the eye of another.

In investigating the background of the Compatibility Quotient questionnaire, we've explored a variety of emotional problems and personality types. Many of these factors may have a bearing on your current relationship, and if they do, by all means begin to act now to make the necessary changes to succeed in marriage—or to extricate yourself from a potentially unhappy or even destructive situation.

Because people and marriages change over time, however, it's important not to regard the CQ as a point-in-time, pass-or-fail test. Rather, what applies to you and your partner today in the CQ may not apply next year or five years from now. Today, you may find yourself dealing with an Emotional Roller Coaster or a Helpless Me. In the future, you may be confronting problems with alcohol or money.

Because things are constantly changing in a marriage, we believe it's helpful for couples to take the CQ more than once over the course of a marriage. In particular, we'd suggest that you pull out the questions once a year, evaluate yourself and your relationship, and make adjustments that may seem appropriate.

Success has been called a journey, and the same might be said of marital compatibility. You're moving toward a destination that might best be characterized as the creative meshing of the interests and egos of two different people into one. Furthermore, you don't have to settle for something far short of this ideal. You can learn not only how to get along and keep the peace with a marriage partner, but how to develop the ability to *enjoy* one another immensely, to work together exuberantly, and to bask in the achievement of common family goals.

In short, even though it may not be possible to reach perfect marital compatibility, we believe quite firmly that it's possible to approach it. The main requirement is a willingness to look deeply within and to have the courage to change when change is clearly in order.